VOM Books
The publishing division of
The Voice of the Martyrs
Serving persecuted Christians since 1967
vom.org

IMPRISONED WITH ISIS

FAITH IN THE FACE OF EVIL

PETR JAŠEK

WITH REBECCA GEORGE

VOMBOOKS
The Voice of the Martyrs

Previously published by Salem Books, an imprint of Regnery Publishing (ISBN 978-1-68451-009-2)

Scriptures marked ESV are taken from THE HOLY BIBLE, ENGLISH STANDARD VERSION®. Copyright © 2001 by Crossway, a publishing ministry of Good News Publishers. Used by permission.

ISBN: 978-0-88264-185-0

Library of Congress Control Number: 2019956082

Published in the United States by
VOM Books, an imprint of
The Voice of the Martyrs
1815 SE Bison Rd.,
Bartlesville, OK 74006
vom.org

Manufactured in the United States of America

To protect the Christians that VOM serves, and especially those Petr served with, certain names or identifying details in this story have been omitted or changed.

202011p004a1

*"For it has been granted to you
that for the sake of Christ you should not only
believe in him but also suffer for his sake ..."*

—PHILIPPIANS 1:29

Contents

Sudan in a Time
of Violent Islamization

While millions in Sudan have struggled to live through extreme poverty, famine, and political instability, those who follow Jesus Christ in a nation governed by Sharia Law and Islamist leaders have long faced a much harsher existence. For three decades, the Sudanese government has targeted Christians, along with those who aren't ethnically Arab, for extermination.

Since former President Omar Hassan al-Bashir rose to power in 1989 through a military coup and established a strict form of Islamic law throughout Sudan, his brutal regime intimidated, arrested, imprisoned, and tortured Christians. It also demolished and bombed church buildings, seeking to further Islamize the country.

In 1993, the United States listed Sudan as a state sponsor of terrorism for harboring members of Islamic terrorist groups, including Osama bin Laden. In 2005, the country's long-running civil war came to a halt with a peace agreement that later resulted in southern Sudan becoming an independent country in 2011. To quell civilian uprisings, Bashir enlisted Arab militias to terrorize civilians in the western Darfur region. As a result, roughly three hundred thousand people were killed and four million more were displaced.

Before the country split, Bashir orchestrated the deaths of nearly two million Christians in southern Sudan, including the Blue Nile region and the Nuba Mountains. In the Nuba region, the Sudanese military dropped more than four thousand bombs on Christian villages, churches, schools, and hospitals to erase all traces of Christianity. Believers there have been treated as criminals and often arrested, tortured, falsely charged, and punished with the death penalty.

In March 2009, The Hague-based International Criminal Court issued an arrest warrant for sixty-five-year-old Bashir—the first warrant ever for a sitting head of state. He was charged with committing war crimes and crimes against humanity, including mass extermination, deportation, torture, and rape in western Sudan. The following year, a second warrant was issued, this time for masterminding genocide in the province of Darfur.

Despite the warrants, Bashir continued to lead Sudan and terrorize Christians until April 11, 2019, when the Sudanese military ousted the dictator following several months of protests.

This story takes place inside Bashir's Sudan a few years before the despot lost his grip on the nation.

Preface

Sunday, May 19, 2013

The heavy steel door slammed shut, caging me inside the suffocating room. The door was speckled with dirty beige paint, and near the top was a window, no larger than five by eight inches. Sitting on the freezing cold floor tiles, I looked at the small rectangle of light and felt forgotten.

My mind darted to my daughter, Vanda—or "Váva," as we call her. She's a beautiful and intelligent young woman who would be graduating from medical school that week. But instead of being with her, celebrating one of the most important moments in her life, I was locked away within this cell. I felt a deep, throbbing sense of shame.

Suddenly, the walls around me began to blur, and the room dissolved into darkness. I felt my heart pounding relentlessly in my chest. Beads of sweat dripped down my forehead and pooled in my eyes, stinging them. I tried to move my limbs, but they didn't respond.

But then I felt a soft sensation. Beneath me was a sheet, a bed, a familiar and comforting place. My arm began to tingle, and I extended it across the bed to feel my wife, also named Vanda, who was sleeping beside me. I saw her long, blonde hair glowing in the rays of the morning dawn. She was as beautiful as she was on the day I married her twenty-three years earlier.

I breathed a sigh of relief and let my head sink back into my pillow. *It was all a terrible dream.* But then the questions began to come. They were like waves lapping against my mind.

Was the dream a message from God? A warning? What could I possibly have done to warrant being arrested and imprisoned?

We crawled out of bed and dressed for church. On that particular Sunday, members of our church in Kladno, in the Czech Republic, were visiting a sister congregation in Karlovy Vary—a quaint spa town near the German border.

Vanda and I got into our car and, along with some friends, embarked on the hour-and-a-half drive west. I said little on the journey through the rambling countryside. My thoughts were filled with questions about my dream.

How did I end up in prison? Did I make a mistake on my taxes?

We arrived at the church early, and I stepped out of the car to shake hands with a church elder who greeted us in the parking lot. He saw that I was distracted.

"Petr, are you all right?"

"I'm all right," I said. But everything inside me felt unsettled. No matter what I said or did, I couldn't shake the feeling I'd had upon waking. I couldn't get the clicking sound of the prison lock out of my head.

For nearly three years, this dream—the most vivid and disturbing of my life—would sleep inside me, waiting to be awakened once again.

1

Two and a half years later

It was shortly before 2:00 a.m. on December 10, 2015. I had been in Sudan for exactly four days, and I couldn't wait to be back home with my family. I felt the familiar emotion of eager anticipation as I thought about my wife, her delicious cooking, and the softness of my bed. In one hour, my flight would depart from Khartoum, so I took a few minutes before leaving my hotel room to use Skype to contact Vanda, who was waiting for me back home in Prague. I smiled as she answered. The call was short, but I hung up anxious to see my wife and ready to begin the journey home.

For more than a decade, I had led the work of The Voice of the Martyrs in Africa. Because my work required me to travel to dangerous places—hostile countries whose Christian citizens endure terrible persecution—Vanda and I established a simple method of communication involving a combination of text messages, phone calls, and Skype video conversations. We also had a series of code words to use if we needed to communicate secretly through letters. My wife and children knew that every trip I took came with a certain measure of risk and that I might encounter any number of perilous situations in the places I visited. But I also tried not to worry my family unnecessarily. I didn't want them to feel scared every time I left home.

On this day, because Vanda would be asleep as I traveled, I would send her a text before my flight departed from Sudan, when I landed in Nairobi, as I departed Nairobi, when I landed in Amsterdam, and as I departed Amsterdam. If everything went smoothly, Vanda would receive a final text as my plane landed on the runway in Prague. She would then drive to the airport to pick me up, synchronizing her arrival to pull the car up to meet me at the exact minute I stepped out of the baggage claim exit.

Since I was traveling as a tourist on this trip, I was wearing casual clothes: a T-shirt and a pair of jeans. A hidden waist belt, one my wife had fashioned, hid my money and second passport. Since my flight left so early, I hadn't slept during the night, but I had showered, and my head was freshly shaved.

I folded my clothes into my carry-on suitcase and opened my laptop bag. It contained my regular passport, driver's license, camera, sunglasses, cell phone, USB drive, external hard drives, and my laptop. A micro-SD chip with encrypted accounting data sat snugly in an interior pocket of my wallet in case my laptop was ever stolen.

The laptop was a state-of-the-art machine, barely a month off the assembly line. My life, and the lives of the persecuted Christians whose stories were documented on the device, depended on my ability to protect it. Between internet sessions, I cleared the browser's cache and deactivated the Wi-Fi to minimize my digital footprint. The laptop never left my side. If someone managed to get their hands on it, they'd only see tourist photos from my recent trip to Nigeria.

But the Nigeria photos were just decoys. The sensitive information—the pictures I had taken the previous night—was encrypted on the laptop's partitioned hard drive, which would be nearly impossible to access.

For the past four days, I had been conducting secret meetings at the Ozone, a bustling open-air café located just opposite the Paradise Hotel where I was staying. With large tan umbrellas shielding the tables and couches, the Ozone had been the perfect place to hold my meetings—one over breakfast, another over lunch, and a final meeting at dinner. Surrounded by expats, including students and professors who taught at various international schools in Sudan, my presence as a white person hadn't appeared unusual.

Before I left the hotel room, I encrypted the remaining photographs and, after erasing them from my camera, transferred the images onto the encrypted partition of my hard drive and took a final sweeping glance over the room. With my carry-on bag in hand and my laptop bag over my shoulder, I walked down the hall and through the lobby. This was just another routine early-morning departure from another hotel for another flight; at least this one would end with me being home.

Fortunately, the roads would be relatively free of traffic at this early morning hour. It would take no more than three minutes for the hotel shuttle to drive me from the hotel to the airport. I scheduled the driver to meet me at precisely 2:00 a.m. to allow one hour for me to check in and clear passport control before my flight departed.

But it was already 2:05, and I was standing outside in the dark. There was no sign of the driver. A few minutes later, I returned to the lobby to ask the receptionist about the delay.

"Someone else is going with you," she said. I walked back outside and waited. Each passing minute felt like a small eternity. No other guest appeared. *Was the receptionist trying to stall me?*

I returned to the reception desk, and she finally summoned the driver. He offered to take my bags, but I handed him only my carry-on suitcase. We climbed into the shuttle, and the driver closed the door behind me. The shuttle lurched into motion.

Just as expected, we arrived at the airport in minutes. I walked into the sparsely populated terminal and headed toward the Kenya Airways desk. The attendant handed me three boarding passes—one for each leg of my trip. I slid two of the boarding passes into my laptop bag and turned toward the line of travelers waiting at passport control. By this time the next day, I would be home from Africa and asleep in my own bed.

Just as I began to move, I felt someone tap me on the shoulder.

"Sudanese security," a man said in stern, broken English. "Please come with us."

2

I was not especially concerned that I had been singled out by the officers. In certain countries I have visited, airport security often conduct quick searches to ensure traveling passengers are not smuggling money out of the country.

This is just a routine screening, I told myself. *After a few short questions and a quick glance through my luggage, I will be on my way to Kenya.*

The two guards were dressed in black trousers and light-colored, short-sleeved, collared shirts. I saw their pistols tucked into their belts as they led me to a small, makeshift interrogation room that had a table and several chairs. The room dividers that served as walls were temporary and grey, and without a ceiling above me, the room filled with noise from the airport terminal.

I glanced down at my watch. If I were going to catch my flight, scheduled to leave in forty-five minutes, I needed to speed up this questioning. The guards were not fluent in English, so I tried speaking to them in French. They stared back at me blankly. Sudan and Russia enjoy a close relationship, so I said a few words to them in Russian. Still, no reaction. Then I tried German—and eventually Czech, my native language. But no matter what I said, my words were met with silence.

"Laptop," one of them ordered in broken English.

I reached into my bag, removed my laptop, and placed it on the table. The guard powered it on and waited for the system to boot. He swiveled the computer to face me and demanded to know the password.

"No way," I said. "It's impossible." I had no intention of making my information easily available to them, even if the hard drive was encrypted.

While the guards fussed with my computer, I quietly unhooked my phone from my belt. My iPhone was programmed to reformat itself after ten failed attempts to enter the correct passcode. I began punching in false PIN numbers, one after the next, hoping to trigger the phone to erase itself. On the fifth attempt, though, the phone froze and required me to wait another five minutes before I could continue. I quickly switched the phone off so that my passcode would be required to open it and my fingerprint wouldn't work—in case they forced me to put my thumb on the button.

One of the guards noticed that I was typing into my phone; I think he suspected I was trying to place a call. He held out his hand and demanded the phone. I glanced to be sure it had completely powered off and handed it to him. He didn't try to turn it back on, at least not then.

"Camera," the guard demanded. I handed him the device, and he began to fidget with it. Above me, in the terminal, I heard the airline attendant paging my name on the airport intercom system. "... *Petr Jašek* ..." I hadn't slept in nearly two days because of my early departure time, and all I wanted was to get on the plane. My level of stress began to rise. "You're delaying my flight," I told the guard, irritation creeping into my tone.

"No problem, no problem," he said in Arabic.

The guard shuffled through a short stack of papers in front of him. "Purpose?" he asked.

"I'm a tourist," I said. The guard carefully examined my passport, tourist visa, and police registration.

Chapter Two

"No tourist," he said. "No tourist."

I checked my watch again. It was 3:00 a.m., and the gate to my plane had surely closed. My flight was leaving without me, and I would have to catch a later one.

I thought of my wife, who would worry if she awoke and discovered no text message from me. I knew that later in the day, my daughter would be taking her final exam for her coursework in internal medicine. I said a prayer for Váva as the guard, who was entirely uninterested in my carry-on suitcase, motioned for my laptop bag and asked me in choppy phrases if I had any other digital storage devices like hard drives or USB drives.

The guard rummaged through my laptop bag and removed the external hard drives and other digital devices. He discovered my second passport, and his eyes lit up.

Because I traveled internationally so often, the Czech government issued me three passports. If I had to send away one in order to receive a visa for an upcoming trip, I was still able to travel with two—one to present to airport security, and one as a backup.

But the guards looked at my second passport and exchanged a knowing glance. *They think I'm a spy.* They took my passports, left the room, and returned with a large, white cell phone.

"Look, look," a guard said, tapping the screen on the phone. "Photo."

I could not believe my eyes. The photograph depicted one of my first meetings with a Sudanese pastor at the Ozone. I worked hard not to give away my surprise with my facial expressions. "It could be me," I said, "but maybe not."

"Name?" the guard asked, pointing to the other man on the screen. I didn't respond.

The guard swiped his finger across the screen and pointed at another photo. "Name!" he insisted.

"What's the problem?" I said, shrugging. "I met some people here."

"What people?"

"I met some friends that I knew before." He swiped again and repeated the questions. I offered no information.

The guards exchanged a few frustrated words in Arabic and left the room. A few minutes later, a sharply dressed officer wearing brown trousers and a yellow checkered jacket walked through the door. He clearly outranked the other men but said nothing, standing silently in the corner of the small room as the guards bombarded me with their fragmented inquiries. My refusal to cooperate had forced them to call their highest ranking officer to the airport. When I continued to skirt their questions, their frustration turned to anger.

By 3:45 a.m., the head security officer realized the interrogation was going nowhere. He unleashed a torrent of Arabic words, and within seconds, the guards gathered their papers and confiscated my carry-on suitcase, my laptop bag, and my wallet.

"You didn't want to cooperate with them," the officer said, gesturing at me. "So now you'll come with us."

3

The situation in which I found myself had actually begun two months earlier when I visited Ethiopia to attend a small conference in the city of Addis Ababa. The week-long event was an opportunity for Christian leaders from the neighboring country of Sudan to consult with, equip, and encourage each other.

At the conference, I met about fifteen Sudanese nationals, over a dozen expats and missionary workers, and others who had been expelled from Sudan several years earlier. The purpose of my trip was to establish new partnerships, to assess the overt persecution of Christians, and to give a ten-minute presentation to pastors and leaders in the area.

At the conference, a pastor named Hassan told me about a young Christian man from Darfur who had been horribly disfigured in Khartoum, the capital city of Sudan, because of his new Christian faith. Nearly a third of the surface of his body—including his face, chest, and hands—had been damaged.

Seeing this young man who had suffered so severely for his faith grieved my heart. I have met many men, women, and children all throughout the world who had suffered tremendous hardships because of their commitment to Jesus Christ. Each time I've met people who bore on their bodies the marks of Christ, I've thanked the Lord for allowing me to work with organizations that help meet the spiritual and physical needs of our persecuted brothers and sisters all over the globe.

"Does he need medical care?" I asked.

"He does," Hassan said. "If you have a chance, could you come to Sudan and speak with him?"

A few days later, I flew back to Prague with the hope of scheduling a quick return trip to Africa to meet this injured Christian. I'd traveled to Sudan more than a dozen times between 2002 and 2011, primarily to the southern part of the country, but I hadn't been there recently. Since the secession of South Sudan in 2011, hostility toward Christians had increased throughout the country.

In January 2005, the Sudan People's Liberation Movement and the official government of Sudan signed a Comprehensive Peace Agreement meant to end an ongoing civil war, develop democracy throughout the country, and equitably divide the profits from the sale of oil. The agreement also established a six-year timetable for working out the details of South Sudan's secession from the North. When 2011 dawned, the two areas of Sudan became two independent countries—Sudan and South Sudan—separated geographically by the Nuba Mountains. Nearly all of the country of Sudan is Muslim, while South Sudan and the Nuba Mountains have large populations of Christians.

There are roughly five million Nuba people in the world today, and approximately 1.5 million of them live in the Nuba Mountains. The rest of them have been driven out, the majority to other parts of Sudan. Since just under half of the Nuba people identify as Christians, they were viewed as a great threat to President Omar al-Bashir and his totalitarian regime. Bashir's goal was the total Islamization and Arabization of Sudan, so the Islamic government in Khartoum, in hopes of eliminating the Nuba people—and their threat to Islamic law—attacked the populace and forbade humanitarian aid in the ninety-mile-wide mountainous region of the Nuba Mountains. Even visiting the area was illegal under his regime.

Bashir felt threatened by the Nuba Mountains because he felt threatened by Christians. Simply by existing, he considered the Nuba people to be committing treason. In the view of the government Bashir established, anyone who tried to shed light on the atrocities committed against the Nuba was committing espionage.

I I I I I I

Acquiring my visa for this trip was easier than I expected. All I needed in order to submit the visa application was a hotel reservation in Sudan, so I reserved a room at the Paradise Hotel in Khartoum and arranged for the staff to register my visit with the local police, as required.

With my room reserved, I drove to Vienna, the closest city with a Sudanese embassy, to apply for a tourist visa, knowing that the request might be denied. I didn't have any other option: As I was applying for the visa, I had no idea if I would be able to meet any of the church leaders on such short notice. There wasn't enough time to arrange for one of the church denominations to provide me with a letter of invitation in order to apply for a religious visa. And apart from the time constraints, it was highly unlikely that the Islamist government of Sudan would grant me a religious-worker visa. Any time I visit a country for the first time, I try to see some of the popular sights in addition to work meetings in order to get to know the country, so I had no qualms about the appropriateness of requesting a tourist visa—I would, in part, be a tourist. There are no guarantees when workers like me enter a country where Christians are persecuted. Every meeting that is planned may happen without incident; on the other hand, there may not be an opportunity to meet with even one Christian due to security concerns or unforeseen circumstances.

At the Sudanese embassy, I presented my hotel and airline ticket reservations, completed the required paperwork, and within two hours, had a tourist visa in hand.

With the trip scheduled, I began contacting the clandestine network of pastors and Christian workers that I had met at the conference in October. Some didn't respond. Others said they would be out of town. But through the process of careful communication, using secure email and avoiding trigger words that might raise suspicion if our messages were intercepted by government officials, I arranged the itinerary for my visit to Khartoum. Several pastors in particular were helpful, especially Pastor Hassan, who is from the Nuba Mountains.

Once I arrived in Khartoum, I was able to visit the ruins of recently demolished churches. To witness a church that has been destroyed, burned to the ground, and bulldozed is always somewhat difficult. It makes me sad for the people of that church and thankful for my own church back home. But I was not that shocked. I oversaw persecution-response projects for years in many nations where Christian churches are often reduced to rubble. In Khartoum, most of these desecrated places of worship were filled with congregations of believers from the Nuba Mountains who have been targeted and heavily persecuted by the Sudanese government. The government claimed the buildings were torn down because the churches were violating zoning laws, but this was only an excuse to persecute Christians; all of the buildings were decades old. The Nuba people had become an official enemy of the Sudanese regime, so they were persecuted politically, culturally, and spiritually. To me, the true reason for this heavy persecution was obvious: these Christians were following Christ's Great Commission to make disciples of all nations, including those under Islamic rule. This was their biggest "crime."

To witness these brave Christians suffering for their faith strengthened my own and solidified my resolve to come to their aid. Their mistreatment by the government frustrated me terribly and saddened me greatly, but I felt well-equipped by my years of experience and VOM's network of contacts to identify ways to help them.

Seeing the ruined buildings paled in comparison to seeing the trauma inflicted upon the individual Christians. On the last day of my trip, I was finally able to meet the young man who needed medical attention, the one Pastor Hassan had told me about in Addis Ababa. The meeting itself, I knew, could jeopardize his safety—and my own as well—so I did not risk inviting him to the Ozone. Instead, we arranged to meet late at night at a private location near where he lived.

The man who would serve as my interpreter was a Christian convert from Islam named Monim. He also was familiar with persecution: after coming to faith in Christ, he'd been arrested and tortured with electric shocks. The security police deliberately arrested him at the time he was supposed to complete his Master's Degree, forcing him to drop out of the program. I admired his courage and was thankful for his language skills.

Monim and I met with a young man named Ali Umar Musa, who had been badly burned in a government attack. I asked about his medical care so far and what other doctors had planned to help him heal from the burns. With Monim's help, I asked Ali to remove his shirt so I could take detailed photos of his injuries. These photos would help doctors working with VOM to advise on the best way to serve him medically.

I also asked Ali about his faith, but he either misunderstood my questions or was reluctant to answer. Monim leaned over and explained quietly that Ali's friends and fellow students, who were sitting in the room with us, had no idea about his new faith. No wonder he didn't want to talk openly about leaving Islam to follow Jesus!

As we left the house where we met Ali, Monim and I arranged another meeting where I later was able to get the full testimony of how he came to believe that Jesus is the Son of God and hear the complete story of his faith. It reminded me of the persecution Christians in Czechoslovakia suffered under Communism when I was young.

After these meetings—I had planned this sensitive conversation to be my last in Sudan—I transferred the photos of Ali's injuries to the encrypted partition on my laptop.

That laptop that was now sitting on the desk being examined by two Sudanese airport security guards.

4

The two guards escorted me out of the interrogation room and led me from the airport to a white Land Cruiser waiting outside. It was one of many that flood the dusty streets of Khartoum. I sat in the backseat for the five-minute drive to the Sudanese National Intelligence and Security Services (NISS) headquarters. The guards took me to a waiting room in the general's office suite, and I sat down on a brown leather sofa. There was no central air or heat, but even at 4:30 in the morning, the temperature in the building still felt pleasant in my jeans and T-shirt.

For hours, I waited. A man holding an AK-47 sat in a chair just outside the room, guarding the exit. His chin fell to his chest, and I wondered whether or not I could escape, but I knew he could wake up at any moment.

Nearly three hours later, two security officers came and retrieved me from the waiting room. "I want to contact the embassy," I told them. "I want to contact my family." They ignored my request and took me to an interrogation room.

"You are working with VOM, right?" the interrogator asked.

I couldn't risk jeopardizing the work I do, so I found ways to respond without giving them information that could be harmful. There were too many Christians in too many countries depending on my ability to navigate this interrogation wisely. Technically, I was not an employee of VOM—I worked as an independent contractor—so I had no trouble answering the interrogator with a confident "No."

He repeated the question.

"I am an advisor to people who want to help the people who suffer," I insisted, emphasizing my background in hospital administration. The interrogator removed a piece of paper from his file and began reading a list of names, pausing after each one.

The names, of course, belonged to pastors I had met the previous October in Ethiopia. My mind flashed back to the conference, back to several Sudanese men I had seen walking around the lobby. Even at the time, I thought they looked suspicious. Now I understood. Those men were government agents—informants sent to gather information about the Christians attending the conference.

I honestly didn't remember the names of all of the people I had met in Addis Ababa, but I refused to give them even the ones I could.

After several minutes, the interrogator closed the file. "If you don't cooperate," he said, "you know we will just have to keep you here longer." He escorted me back to the suite, and for hours, I waited on the sofa.

When the Sudanese Security officer finally led me back into the interrogation room, I saw my laptop sitting open on the table, next to my external hard drives and camera. Before my trip to Sudan, I had transferred photos from my old laptop to my new one. I was 100 percent certain that I had deleted all the photos from my external hard drive, and during the questioning, I was not concerned about the content safely protected on the computer's encrypted partition. I was sure the devices were clean.

But the next thing I heard sent a chill down my spine.

The interrogator tapped a button on my laptop, and I heard the sound of a familiar voice come blaring through the speakers. *Now we are in the Nuba Mountains . . .* The voice belonged to a ministry colleague.

Why is there a video from 2011 on my external hard drive?

Chapter Four

In 2012, at the beginning of the second war in the hotly contested Nuba Mountains, I traveled along with other Christian leaders to the Nubas to document it and offer relief to persecuted Christians. Like me, they have conducted Christian mission work in the mountainous region separating Sudan from South Sudan for years—work the Bashir administration considered illegal.

One of our flights delivering aid into the Nuba Mountains was the last allowed to land before the airspace was closed and the airstrip bombed. In the years since 2011, the Sudanese government has continued to restrict this type of aid work, and they prosecute offenders harshly. For more than fifteen years, on orders from President Bashir, the Nuba Mountains were continuously bombed, but only recently had the United Nations listened to the people reporting these bombings— people like the friend speaking in the video I was now watching.

But how did this video get onto my laptop?

Next, the prosecutor laid on the table a photograph of two men sitting casually inside the fuselage of an airplane. I immediately recognized it. As I took a closer look, I noticed a caption had been written across the bottom: "Heading for the war zone."

Suddenly, everything became terrifyingly clear. The NISS had managed to restore the deleted videos and photos from my external hard drives—the ones I used to transfer videos and photos from my previous laptop to the encrypted partition of my new laptop's hard drive. They had also found a way to restore the deleted images of Ali's body that I had taken on the final night of my trip, just before I was arrested.

"What is this man's name?" the interrogator asked, pointing at a picture of the young Christian student. I refused to respond, wondering how they could have accessed the deleted pictures. Then I felt a chill creep from my spine up my neck and a terrible sinking feeling in the pit of my stomach as I realized what had happened. *I deleted the photos, but I failed to overwrite the camera's SD memory card with the special program that would prevent the files from being restored.*

The man pulled out a piece of paper and began reading a list of names that I immediately recognized from the contacts in my Skype account. The NISS had accessed my account and was using my contacts to connect me to workers at VOM and other Christian ministries.

I knew now I was definitely in deep trouble. The Sudanese government might very well have a strong case against me because, under their oppressive laws, those who do this kind of Christian work are seen not only as spies but also as enemies of the state.

5

Several hours later, I was brought back to the interrogation room and saw photos spread out across the table. There were dozens— photographs of me entering the Paradise Hotel, exiting the hotel, walking through the lobby, eating at the Ozone, visiting a demolished church. Over the previous four days, Sudanese government agents had been watching me, following me, and documenting every single one of my activities in Khartoum. The interrogator drew my attention to a set of green-tinted photographs that had been taken with a night vision camera. They have been following me day and night. I was alarmed and more than a little worried, but I worked hard to maintain a calm outward appearance.

Finally, the interrogator pulled out an SD card and laid it triumphantly on the table. The memory card was a password-protected copy of my accounting documents. I kept it in my wallet when I traveled to make sure that my financial information was up to date. To the NISS interrogator, however, the card was further evidence that I was a spy.

"Please allow me contact with the embassy," I said again. "Allow me contact with my family."

Without answering, the interrogator walked me back to the waiting room, then retrieved me several hours later for another few minutes of questioning. This routine continued for the rest of the day and well into the night. In frustrated silence, I waited, knowing how worried Vanda would be, wondering how bad my situation really was. To break up the monotony and to let me stretch my legs, the interrogator allowed me to move to a stairwell landing. It was approaching midnight, but the NISS building was still bustling with activity, and I watched the employees ascending and descending the stairs.

As I waited, I thought about my parents, who endured years of persecution for being Christians in Communist Czechoslovakia. I was born into a Christian family in the 1960s, when my country was still part of the so-called Eastern Bloc of the Soviet Union. In the decade before my birth, Christians suffered horrific torture, imprisonment, and often death throughout Communist-occupied Europe. It was a time when the government persecuted us greatly and outlawed the practice of our faith outside approved, government-controlled churches.

Because my father was a pastor, our family moved quite frequently. When I was in the fourth grade, we again moved to a new town. It was very difficult to move to a new area during the school year because my classmates would always ask me, "What does your dad do?"

It's a very natural question, but I was afraid to tell the truth. I was afraid that my classmates would laugh at me if they knew my dad was a pastor, so I said he was a beekeeper. My answer wasn't *entirely* a lie because, as a hobby, my dad did keep beehives. But deep down in my heart, I knew I had lied, and my mind always returned to that story in the Bible when another Peter—Simon Peter, the disciple of Christ—denied Him by saying he didn't know the man (Luke 22:54–62).

This knowledge, that I had denied Christ, followed me through childhood. I felt ashamed. When I became a Christian and began to follow Christ at the age of fifteen, I made a conscious decision never to deny my Savior again.

Chapter Five

When I was in high school, secret police visited my father's church often. They followed his ministry, monitored him, and then reported his Christian activities to the government. In addition to their work in the church, my parents also led a secret "underground" discipleship training program for young people around the country. One day, I came home from school and realized that both of my parents had been arrested. The secret police interrogated them thoroughly before releasing them.

Because of those experiences, my father taught me how to behave during interrogation. He taught me the importance of answering questions consistently and verbatim because interrogators would often ask the same questions again later to detect any difference between the two answers. He also taught me to carefully distinguish between information the interrogator *already knows* and the information *he wants to know.*

I didn't know what the next day would hold, and I felt ill-equipped for what lay ahead, but I took comfort in God's promise to David in the book of Psalms: "The Lord preserves the simple; when I was brought low, he saved me" (Psalm 116:6).

As I meditated on the Psalm, I noticed a man walking toward me on the stairwell. He had gray hair and a long gray beard, and his skin was light, more Arab than Sudanese. I had seen him before. He'd been sitting in the lobby of the Churchill Hotel in Addis Ababa two months earlier. A sobering thought dawned on me:

The Sudanese Security knew everything about me before I even entered the country.

6

While I was being interrogated in the Khartoum airport, my wife, Vanda, was at our home in Prague 2,600 miles away, waiting anxiously to receive an update from me.

When 7:30 a.m. came and went, Vanda began to worry. She should have received a text from me before my flight departed Sudan at 2:00 a.m. her time. At the very latest, she should have heard from me, either by text or Skype, by 7:30 a.m. as my flight left Nairobi for Amsterdam. *Has Petr missed his flight?* she wondered. Vanda knew I was scheduled to land in Prague at 5:30 p.m., but as evening approached, there was still no word. She checked the airline schedules and saw there were two more incoming flights from Amsterdam later that night, with the last scheduled to arrive at 10:30 p.m.

Vanda grew up a nominal Catholic, the granddaughter of a farmer who had been imprisoned for resisting Communist efforts to seize his land. For all of her early life, she had been uninterested in knowing or following God. In her early twenties, though, Vanda began working in a hospital—in the same department where I worked.

One day, I deliberately left a Bible in an on-call room so I could read it during my shifts. Over the weeks, I suspected that someone else was reading it as well. When the department supervisor demanded that the Bible disappear, Vanda approached me and asked for a Bible of her own.

In November 1989, as the walls of Communism began to crumble in Czechoslovakia during the Velvet Revolution, the walls around Vanda's heart began to crumble as well. In time, she became a Christian. When I became a Christian at a summer camp in East Germany at the age of fifteen, I knew I never wanted to marry or raise children under Communism. This all changed, however, as I found myself captivated by this bold, beautiful woman and her blossoming Christian faith.

Over time, Vanda and I forged a close connection and spent hours talking about the Gospel and our shared commitment to Jesus Christ. Our friendship soon grew into a relationship of love, and on April 6, 1990, we exchanged our marriage vows. As is the custom in our country, after our wedding, Vanda became Vanda "Jašková"—a surname with a suffix that, in Czech, means "belonging to."

Vanda had entrusted herself to me, and together, we entrusted our future to Christ, no matter the cost.

I   I   I   I   I   I

On the day of my interrogation, Váva completed her final exam in Internal Medicine and then spent the evening celebrating with friends. Shortly after 10:30 p.m., though, she received a concerned text message from her mother. Her father was missing. Váva hurried home.

She and her brother tried to reassure Vanda. "Maybe he did not have a chance to call," they said. "Maybe his connection time was tight."

Because she is fluent in English, Váva was tasked with making phone calls—but she had no specific protocol to follow if I went missing. Whenever I traveled, I always left my hotel reservation and flight information with Vanda. My wife's first phone call was to our pastor. Immediately, our church began a prayer chain, with different members of the congregation signing up to pray specifically for me so that prayers were being offered to God on my behalf around the clock. Váva alerted VOM staff members that her father had not arrived and then called the Czech police. "My father was coming back from Sudan," she said, "and he didn't arrive at the airport. We don't know what happened."

Váva and Vanda filed a report at the Czech police station. The officer asked for details about our family's finances, my contact information, our family history and relatives, and any connection that could help locate me. Finally, the police added my name to Interpol's list of missing people.

Through the night, my family searched online for suggestions about what to do next. The following morning, Váva called the Sudanese Embassy in Vienna but was unable to make headway. She hung up and called the Czech Embassy in Cairo, which oversees Czech interests in Sudan as well. But because it was Friday, a weekly day of rest for Egyptian government offices, no one answered the phone, so she left a voicemail message and phoned the Czech Ministry of Foreign Affairs in Prague.

"Our father is missing," she said. "I need help."

Surprisingly, the Czech ambassador in Cairo returned Váva's phone call on Friday afternoon and asked for the details surrounding my trip.

"What was he doing in Sudan?" the ambassador asked. Váva said I was a tourist.

"Are there any conflicts you know of that could have caused him to be arrested?"

"We are a Christian family," Váva said, giving the name of our church in Prague. The ambassador hung up the phone with a promise to try to find some information about me.

Váva soon abandoned the cover story that I was a tourist because Sudan is not a country people typically visit for sightseeing. Besides, it would be strange for a father to travel by himself on vacation without his wife or children.

Throughout the day, between the countless phone calls, Váva and my son, Petr, prayed with Vanda. My deputy director with VOM arrived at our home and immediately went to work making phone calls with Váva.

They called the Paradise Hotel in Khartoum and learned that I had departed for the airport on the shuttle just after 2 a.m. Then they called the shuttle driver, but since the man spoke only Arabic, they were unable to glean any information. The Kenya Airways representative reported that I had checked in for my flight but had not boarded the plane.

My last known location was the Khartoum airport, so my family knew I likely hadn't been kidnapped. Vanda now feared an equally alarming reality: I was in the custody of the Sudanese government.

7

Just after midnight, a guard roused me from my light sleep on the sofa in the general's office and took me once again to the interrogation room. I quickly struggled to make my mind and body alert. An officer entered the room with a folder in hand. He summoned three guards, showed them the contents of the folder, and signed his name to a piece of paper. When I saw him close the folder and hand it to one of the guards, I knew what was about to happen.

I'm going to prison. The folder full of forms and the pictures of those I'd met with in Khartoum told me they weren't going to just question me until the next flight left. They'd put in too much work to merely delay me until a later flight. I was being detained. And my stay probably wasn't going to be short.

My carry-on suitcase and clothes were returned to me; the interrogators kept my two passports, ID cards, driver's license, and the laptop bag and its contents.

Two heavily armed guards loaded me into the backseat of a small white Kia. One sat in the passenger seat beside the driver. The other man sat next to me with a machine gun in his hands.

After a twenty-minute drive, the car ground to a halt next to a relatively small, nondescript, four-story building—the NISS facility for political prisoners. The guards escorted me inside and handed my folder to the chief prison official. The man began the slow process of admitting me into the prison.

"When did you study in primary school?" the official asked. This was an odd question, but it was not one that surprised me. I knew the Sudanese Security officer would likely try to gather as much information as possible about me, my family, and the people I knew. I was familiar with this type of questioning—it was similar to what Communist officials asked when arresting people in Czechoslovakia. I took a deep breath to steady my nerves.

I did not intend to offer the official any information he might use against me, so I stayed silent. When I refused to answer, he stared silently at me. At this point, I had been awake for forty-eight hours and was exhausted. I realized the official intended to wait until I answered, so I offered a few random dates, which he recorded.

"What is your mother's name?" he continued.

"My mother passed away eighteen years ago," I said, but he insisted on having her maiden name anyway. I determined that there was little chance of the information being incriminating, so I answered.

The official looked down at the paper in front of him, searching for the next question. "Who are the parents of three of your relatives?" These questions continued for some time, and I supplied half-hearted, often inaccurate answers to speed up the process. My watch had been confiscated, and I wasn't certain of the exact time. It must have been at least 1:00 a.m.

The official finished his questions and handed me over to a prison photographer. As he took mugshots of me from the front and the side, I again got the feeling that my stay here would be much longer than one night.

Before I surrendered my carry-on suitcase, a prison guard allowed me to remove a few articles of clothing: one extra pair of pants, two extra shirts, some underwear, and a pair of socks. I took my soap, toothbrush, and toothpaste, but the guards forbade me from bringing my belt or light summer jacket into the prison. I usually traveled with an extra towel when I visited Africa, but because I had booked a room at the Paradise Hotel, I saw no need to bring it on this trip. It was a decision I was beginning to regret.

The guards led me and another newly minted prisoner to an elevator that took us to the third floor. The silent hallway was mostly dark; looking up, I saw that most of the light bulbs were broken. I saw rectangles of light spilling from some of the small windows in cell doors as we walked. Keeping the hallway dark and the individual cells fully lit allowed the guards to see what went on in each cell and prevented the prisoners from seeing the guards in the hallway.

At one particular cell, the guards paused. One of them unlocked the door and ushered the prisoner beside me into the overcrowded room. I started to follow him but was instructed to wait.

Further down the corridor, we stopped at another cell. The guard unlocked the door and motioned for me to step inside. Harsh, fluorescent light filled the room, shining on five men lying on the floor. A sixth man was stretched out on the lone metal bed. As I entered, the prisoners stirred. These cells had been designed for one inmate per cell; the designers never planned for seven men to share such a small space.

As I watched the guards turn to leave, my eyes lingered on the dirty beige paint speckled across the heavy metal door. I heard the automatic lock click into place as the guard closed the door behind him.

I knew that sound. I knew this cell. I had been here before.

Only this time, it wasn't a dream.

8

I surveyed my new surroundings and wondered how seven of us were going to share a cell that was, at most, eight feet wide and fourteen feet long. The walls were filthy, and insects—ants, flies and mosquitos—infested the room. There was a short, swinging wooden door that cordoned off the toilet and shower area, and I could smell mold growing near the primitive bathroom. The shower was completely broken, and the Western-style metal toilet was covered in rust. There was a hose coming out of the wall, but I would quickly learn that the water was only on once or twice a day, and it was sometimes off for a whole week. I learned to keep bottles and to fill them up any time the water was flowing.

The one bed in the room, a rusty metal frame, ate deeply into the space, as did the desk with its accompanying chair. A strong stench of body odor filled the room. I felt my stomach sink as the reality of my new situation set in. *How long will I have to endure this?*

The men on the floor had mattresses and blankets, and they squeezed closer together to make a little bit of space for me to lie down near the entrance to the toilet. Without a mattress beneath me, the dirty tile floor sent a chill through my thin T-shirt. I created a makeshift blanket using both of my extra shirts. With one, I covered my upper body, and I wrapped the other around my legs. They did little to guard against the December draft. I wondered if I would get sick. The severe overhead light flooded the room as I thought about my wife and children. *How worried they must be.* The anxiety I felt sat in the pit of my stomach like a rock.

There, curled up on the frigid floor in this overcrowded, filthy cell, I attempted a few hours of sleep.

| | | | | | |

At roughly 4:30 a.m., I was jolted awake by the *azaan*, the loud chanting of the morning call to prayer. The sound started somewhere in the prison before the first rays of dawn and spread from cell to cell, waking each Muslim. I was on high alert.

The men around me rose to their feet and began performing their morning ablutions. The men in my cell had long beards but only short stubble where a mustache would have been. It was a look I had seen before among extremists in other Muslim countries. I saw that most of them were wearing long, flowing *jalabiya*, the robes common among Arabic men, and I moved out of the way so they could access the tall *ibrig* of water in our bathroom. The spouted plastic bottle didn't look clean, but I knew that without this ritual washing, my Muslim cellmates wouldn't be able to do their morning prayers.

"When we pray," one of my cellmates told me in English, "you have to wake up and stand here." He pointed at the back corner of the room. "We cannot face you."

From the corner of the room, I watched as each man bowed to a half-filled bottle of water in front of him. Each time, they lowered their torsos toward the floor and hit something I could not see. They repeated this movement more than a dozen times as their chanted prayers filled the room.

When they finished, the men returned to their mattresses because of the limited space to walk around in the room. The ones who spoke English began to ask me questions.

Chapter Eight

"What country are you from, and why are you here?"

"I am from the Czech Republic," I said. "I was leaving the country after a four-day visit when the Sudanese security arrested me at the airport and confiscated my laptop, camera, and phone."

"What is your business?"

Because I am a white European, I knew they likely suspected that I was a Christian, but I didn't tell them my true agenda—that I came on this trip to meet Sudanese pastors. Instead, I told them about my private consulting company in healthcare administration and explained that I came to Sudan as a tourist.

"We have no newspapers," someone said. "What is new in the world?"

The first thing that came to mind was the November 13 terrorist attack in Paris, which had happened less than a month earlier. "Through coordinated attacks in several places around the city," I explained, "one hundred twenty-nine people died." I added that ISIS had claimed responsibility for the suicide bombings and mass shootings.

The room fell suddenly silent—then erupted with frenetic shouts of *"Allahu Akbar!"* I sucked in a quick, startled breath. My eyes widened. The men jumped up from the floor and embraced each other in jubilant hugs. They raised their arms in triumph and danced around our crowded cell, slapping each other on the back and smiling. I inched toward the closest wall, my hands becoming suddenly clammy. Beads of sweat rose on my upper lip and forehead, and I tried not to shake.

For several minutes, my cellmates celebrated the successful terrorist attack in France. I had seen this kind of Muslim celebration on television, but to experience it for the first time in person was shocking.

I realized, in those terrifying moments, that I had been imprisoned with Islamic extremists. In the coming days, I would learn that my cellmates were in fact members of ISIS.

9

One of my cellmates had been trained as a pharmacist. He spoke excellent English and explained to me that he'd been arrested in Turkey trying to cross into Syria, where he planned to offer his medicinal expertise in service to the "Caliphate." I would soon discover that he wasn't the only one of my cell mates with such loyalties. They used the Arabic acronym *"Daesh"* to refer to the Islamic State.

Though Sudan's government is an Islamist Sunni government, they did not want to see ISIS (also Sunni Muslims) spread within its borders. Bashir's government feared that if the group was allowed to grow unchecked, it might one day rival the government's own hold over Sudan's people. The government was also working to improve diplomatic relations with certain Western governments, and being seen as an "ally" in the "war on terror" was a key part of those efforts.

Five times each day, I stood in the corner of my room and witnessed my Muslim cellmates—all of them members of ISIS or sympathizers—bow their faces in prayer. A half-filled bottle of water was placed on the floor of the cell to point the direction to Mecca so they could properly "aim" their prayers. The extremists were the first to rise every morning, pulling blankets off the more nominal

Muslims, waking them with deafening shouts of "*Salah. Salah!*" During the prayers, they stood behind the others to correct their posture and show them where their feet should go and how to bow properly. As I watched them give instructions on how to correctly interpret the Koran, it became obvious to me that my devoutly Islamist cellmates were busy recruiting and radicalizing the others to join their cause. I oscillated between feelings of sadness for their souls and concern for the hatred they fostered, even from our tiny, locked cell. There were three or four copies of the Koran in our cell, so over and over again, I asked the guards for a Bible. Usually, they just laughed.

Islam forbids artwork that depicts the faces of people or animals, so my cellmates had smeared pink toothpaste over the walls in our room to cover up the drawings left by previous prisoners. There was never enough food to satisfy our ravenous appetites.

We ate our meals together, scooping food from the same bowl with bare hands. Because many Sudanese don't use toilet paper and because my cellmates rarely washed their hands thoroughly with soap after using the toilet—partly because the water was only on once or twice a day—I lost much of my appetite. I tried not to offend them and picked at my meals, but each day I felt myself growing thinner and weaker. To stave off infection, I bathed myself with two liters of water and the red carbolic soap issued by the prison, and I washed my hands as often as I could. The smell reminded me of the disinfectant used in the hospitals in Czechoslovakia in the 1960s.

The pharmacist wasn't the only one of my cellmates loyal to ISIS; several of them had traveled to Syria to fight as radical jihadis. Others wanted to go there but hadn't yet succeeded. They were imprisoned here at the NISS prison for radicalism and for committing a variety of other crimes: changing money unofficially, trading weapons or gold illegally, or selling gasoline without an official receipt.

On sunny days, I felt hopeful and comforted by the beams of light that seeped through a blurred-glass window near the ceiling of one of the walls. Even though I could not see the courtyard beyond my cell, the window offered me a beautiful view to the outdoors. On clear days, I could see the sun for about fifteen minutes in the morning, which refreshed my spirit. When the sun shifted, however, the cell was once again enveloped in shadows. I was cold all the time.

One day, I looked through the small window in the door and saw a guard walk by.

"May I have a blanket?" I asked, rapping on the door to attract his attention.

The guard stopped and smirked. "You are from Czech Republic," he said. "You are used to cold weather. No blanket for you." My only hope was that one of the other prisoners would be released, and when he was, I might inherit his dirty, pungent blanket.

A week into my imprisonment, the man who slept on the one bed in our cell approached me. His family had just brought him a second brand-new blanket—a soft, flannel one with yellow and orange flowers—and he had decided to give it to me.

"This is for you," he said with tears in his eyes. I was moved by his gift, and I felt the emotion welling in my own eyes. For the first time since I arrived in prison, I would finally be warm. This kind gesture overwhelmed me. Even in the midst of this terrible situation, I was reminded of God's care and provision. He had answered my prayer.

"I don't have anything to reimburse you," I told him. "What can I do?"

What he said next took me by surprise. "Pray for me," he said.

"Can I pray for you to find the right way to God?"

"Yes," he said, "please pray that I can find the right way to God."

Four days later, he was released from prison, and I never saw him again.

| | | | | | |

In 2012, Salah Abdallah Gosh, the director of Sudan's NISS, had overseen the construction of the four-story prison that was now my home. The top two floors held roughly forty cells. Below them was a floor of offices, and the ground floor was reserved for interrogations and torture. The square building was relatively modern, but by the time I arrived, it was already in a terrible state of disrepair. In November 2012, the same year the building was completed, Gosh was accused of plotting a coup to overthrow President Omar al-Bashir. He found himself imprisoned for six months in the facility he himself had built.

This NISS prison was built according to a British model, and I was told that the metal elements like beds, tables, and toilets, and some of the other materials were actually imported from the UK. However, the construction was subpar. The insulation was ineffective for keeping out humidity, and the water rarely flowed. There was an air conditioner, but I was told that, during the summer months, it was unable to maintain a consistent temperature. Muslims were able to secure water for their ablutions, but there was almost never enough running water for showering.

Though the British had designed these cells for one prisoner apiece, Sudanese prison authorities "adapted" the cells for more men, usually seven. But when they had prisoners from Darfur and the Nuba Mountains—the supposed enemies of Bashir's regime—they put up to fifteen prisoners in one cell. When my cellmates told me there had recently been an influx of prisoners, I was thankful there were "only" seven of us in the one room.

Whenever I traveled, I took with me a bottle of a headache relief medicine—a combination of aspirin, acetaminophen, and caffeine. The guards evidently had found it in my suitcase and determined that I should receive regular doses of it. I found the guards' commitment to this somewhat humorous—if anything, it would likely cause more harm than good. But each day, since I was suffering from dehydration-induced morning headaches, they brought me one tablet of the medicine, and I dutifully swallowed it. I hoarded the Imodium and Malarone (anti-malarial) they also had ferreted from my suitcase for the future in case I would really need these medicines.

Sudanese law allowed the NISS to detain inmates for varying periods of time without a court trial or verdict. Money changers and gold smugglers, for example, could be held for four months. ISIS sympathizers, like my cellmates, could be kept for up to a year.

Day by day, I listened to their stories and looked for ways to share the love of Jesus with them. One afternoon, several of the men were boasting about some pastors from America who were convinced by the Muslim people to adopt Islam. This errant and syncretistic hybrid of Christianity and Islam, sometimes referred to as *Chrislam*, had spread in some countries in Europe and the Middle East. "This is the true religion," my ISIS cellmate claimed.

Sure, there are some Christians—often more nominal, cultural Christians than devout believers in Jesus Christ—who decided to follow the tenets of Islam. But I knew there were far more people— hundreds of thousands in nations all around the world—who had forsaken Muhammed and were now following Jesus Christ. I didn't want to start an argument, but I did hope to at least plant a seed that would make my cellmates think.

"I meet other people," I replied. "Courageous Christians from Nigeria." I was thinking of the story of a young woman named Monica.

In July 2009, Monica and her husband were riding a motorcycle through the city of Maiduguri in Northern Nigeria. It was a Thursday, and they were on their way to church to attend a Bible study. As they traveled, though, Islamic militants wearing camouflaged military uniforms and masks flooded the road and blocked their path. The men carried long, sharp machetes and machine guns. Monica and her husband knew these men were members of Boko Haram, the jihadi terrorist group that had been rampaging northern Nigeria.

"What is your religion?" one of the militants demanded, stepping forward menacingly with his machete in his hand.

"We are Christians," Monica and her husband boldly replied.

"You can save your lives by becoming Muslims," the militant said. "Repeat the *shahada*," he insisted, referring to the Muslim profession of faith. But the two Christians refused.

"We are Christians," they said, "and we remain Christians."

The Boko Haram militant raised his machete and, in three swift slices, severed Monica's husband's head from his body. Knowing her husband was dead and that there was nothing she could do to help him, she ran. The men chased her, slicing at her back with a sharp machete. Soon, she felt a heavy hand on her shoulder.

She had been caught.

The angry militant spun her around and sliced her throat with his machete. Monica fell to the ground, blood gushing from her neck, and within seconds, she lost consciousness. The men, assuming she was dead as well, tossed her body into a sewer where she lay for the next two and a half hours. As she was lying unconscious in the ditch, she saw heavenly beings dressed in white surrounding her.

Finally, members of the village police came through to identify the victims of Boko Haram's most recent attack and bury the bodies. They spotted Monica and lifted her from the ditch, but to their surprise, she started to move. Using sign language, she asked for some water. One of the policemen gave her water to drink, but it dribbled out through the cut in her throat.

The police took Monica to the local hospital, where she underwent several surgeries. Doctors implanted a device in her throat through a tracheotomy so she could breathe; when covering the hole in the device with her finger, she could even speak in a whisper.

I remembered clearly the first time I met Monica. VOM had sent me to see how we might offer medical aid to her. I was deeply moved by the story of her husband's murder and the vicious attack against her and the boldness with which they both had declared their faith in Christ. My colleague from the Mayo Clinic in the US was reviewing her medical history as I prepared questions for my interview and documented her injuries with my camera. I felt a tremendous burden for her and struggled to find the right way to begin my interview.

Eventually, I dared to ask her a simple question: "Monica," I asked, "how are you doing in the Lord? How has your relationship with the Lord changed after this horrific experience?"

I will never forget her answer. Before she could speak, Monica took a deep breath then closed the hole in her throat device with her index finger so air could pass through her damaged vocal cords. Finally, in a raspy voice modulated by the device in her throat, she whispered: "I focus my eyes on eternity." She removed her finger, took another deep breath, and then continued. "I focus my eyes on Jesus."

Through breathy, pained whispers, Monica told me that before the attack, she had considered herself and her husband "good" Christians. But she had been concerned with buying a new dress and working hard to save money to buy a nice car or house. Now, after her husband's death and her own miraculous deliverance, she wanted to dedicate her whole life to serving Jesus. In fact, soon after her final surgery, Monica began the dangerous, brave work of helping VOM assist other widows who have lost their husbands in attacks like the ones committed by Boko Haram militants. Twice, VOM has had to relocate her when her life was in danger.

I wanted the men in my cell to know Monica's story because it is a powerful testimony of faith in Jesus Christ, so I began telling them. As soon as I described her husband's head being severed from his body, though, the ISIS men in my cell stopped me. The pharmacist— an intelligent man with a young daughter—began to laugh. It was an unsettling, evil, gleeful sound that I would never be able or willing to imitate, and I knew not to share any more stories of Christian persecution with the ISIS militants in my cell. In a situation in which I would have expected even a minimum of human sympathy for a woman who had lost her husband in such a horrific way and who was badly injured as well, these young, educated ISIS members were instead laughing and saying, *"Allahu Akbar."*

| | | | | | |

Late at night, I overheard my cellmates praying over the *mujahedin* guerrilla fighters in Libya, Iraq, and Syria. They were speaking in Arabic, but I was able to decipher enough words and phrases to piece together their requests. They were praying for success and favor from Allah, but these were unlike the required, scripted prayers I heard them recite throughout the day. These were their private prayers, expressed in their own words.

On another occasion, I was awakened by the loud sneezes of the pharmacist who, because of his sore and stuffy nose, had been unable to sleep. Instead, he had decided to pray. I saw him on his knees with his arms lifted up, tears flowing from his eyes as he silently prayed to be released and to be reunited with his young family. On various nights, other members of ISIS woke and prayed similar prayers, fervently lifting their requests to Allah in their own words.

I was encouraged by these signs of tenderness in my cellmates, and my heart yearned for them to know God. In other countries like Egypt, I had met former Muslim extremists who had become believers. Seeing the vulnerability and humanity of these ISIS militants gave me hope, and I decided to focus many of my prayers on asking Jesus Christ to reveal Himself to them as Lord, Savior, and God.

As the days went by, one agonizing day after another, I wondered if the Lord would change the hearts of my ISIS cellmates or if I would suffer at their hands there in the Sudanese cell.

10

A week and a half after my arrest, I still hadn't been allowed to call the Czech Embassy in Cairo or my family at home in the Czech Republic. All I had been able to do was wait and pray. Waiting was a crucial component of the NISS interrogation strategy. The longer you had to wait, they presumed, the more likely you would be to answer their questions. To a fledgling prisoner like me, waiting was excruciating torture. Ten days felt like an agonizing eternity. Thoughts of Vanda filled every crevice of my mind, and I knew she must be worried sick about me. *Does she even know where I am?* I coped by turning my thoughts to God, by praying, and by anticipating my return home.

My next interrogation finally took place on December 20. I was led from my cell down to the first floor of the prison where I was met by a man I recognized—it was the high-ranking Sudanese NISS officer from the airport, the man who spoke English and was called to make the final decision about my arrest. I expected him to ask me questions about Pastor Hassan, brother Monim, and the Muslim convert to Christ whom I interviewed, but with the evidence the NISS retrieved from their surveillance, coupled with the deleted photos and videos from my camera's SD card, he apparently saw no need to ask such questions.

Instead of questioning me, he handed me a piece of paper. I was surprised to see what appeared to be a short script written in English. I scanned the paper and could not believe my eyes—I would finally be able to call my family! Since the moment I was pulled aside in the Khartoum airport, I had been begging to contact my family. My wife and children had had no communication with me at all. At last, I would be able to let them know I was doing okay. My heart raced, and the paper in my hand began to shake as feelings of exhilaration and sheer relief filled my heart.

The interrogator handed me a telephone and I dialed the only number I could remember, my wife's cell phone. I would have thirty seconds to recite only the words on the script and nothing more.

"Only English," the man insisted. "Only English!"

The call was dispatched, and I heard the sound of a telephone ringing. "This is my wife's number," I told him, "and she doesn't speak English. She might hand the phone over to our daughter."

When the call connected, I heard Vanda's voice. "It is me," I said quickly in Czech, "but I have to speak only English."

"Petr, is it you?" she cried. She immediately handed the phone to Váva and I recited my script.

"I am all right," I said, reading the script. I knew my voice was shaking, and I tried to steady it. "There has been a little misunderstanding, and I have been arrested, but I will try to be in touch with you soon."

"We have contacted the embassy in Cairo," my daughter said, "and everybody is praying for you."

"I'm all right," I repeated. "I will try to be in touch with you soon."

At the end of the thirty-second call, I went off script. "I love you," I told her. I could hear Váva crying, and my heart broke. The prosecutor motioned to me and reluctantly, I hung up the phone. The call was hardly enough to satisfy the deep longing for my family, but at least they knew I was alive. I felt my chest tighten and my eyes brim with tears as the guard led me back to my cell.

❙   ❙   ❙   ❙   ❙   ❙

The next day, December 21, a guard came to my cell and told me I had a visitor. The news was a shock. The visitor was not allowed to meet with me in the prison building, so the guards prepared to transfer me. I felt optimistic and hopeful as they handcuffed me with heavy chains attached to my wrists and ankles. They led me outside to a minibus, and I climbed awkwardly into the vehicle as six men— two armed with AK-47s and the other four with smaller guns—joined me for the forty-five minute drive to a building called the National Club, a special NISS facility in Khartoum surrounded by beautifully landscaped gardens. It seemed as if the Sudanese viewed me as a high-profile prisoner. The handcuffs cut deep grooves into my wrists.

The NISS must have known about the upcoming visit from the office of the consul general of the Czech Embassy, which explained the phone call the day before. They needed to be able to report to the consular officer that they had allowed me to contact my family. When the vehicle finally came to a stop, the guard next to me walked me into the building. He removed my handcuffs, but the painful marks on my wrists remained.

The consular officer was a white man in a suit and tie named Štěpán Sláma, an official appointed by the Czech government to live in Cairo and protect the interests of Czech citizens in the region. He had traveled from Egypt to meet with me. When I realized who he was, I was so relieved I could have wept, and I was even more thrilled when I realized we would be able to conduct the entire conversation in Czech.

"Your family is aware of your detention," Mr. Sláma said, reassuringly, "and they are doing well."

I sighed deeply and told him about the photos and videos the Sudanese Security had been able to recover from my external hard drive, especially the video they played of the Nuba Mountains. I wondered how this would complicate the case, so I carefully spelled out the word

Nuba for him using the Czech alphabet. He told me that the NISS would transfer my case to a court within one month and that the preliminary reports were that I had been accused of smuggling tiger hides.

I laughed incredulously at the absurd charge. *Are there even any tigers in Sudan?*

The Sudanese had recently brought charges against a Swiss missionary, several Americans, and a Korean pastor—other people who, in recent times, had also been arrested in Sudan for various types of Christian work. Those charges, Mr. Sláma explained to me, were usually resolved within about three or four months. I was glad to hear this, but I also knew that it meant I likely wouldn't be home with my family in time for Christmas.

Ever since I had arrived at the NISS prison ten days earlier, my digestive system had been tied up in knots. So far, I hadn't even used the toilet fully since I had been incarcerated with the members of ISIS, and my stomach ached. But as the meeting concluded and I left the National Club, I felt encouraged by my visit with the consular officer. He had been a warm, friendly presence, trying to put my mind at ease while at the same time offering realistic expectations about my case, and I felt a huge sense of relief. It was extremely comforting to realize that I was not alone. *The Czech government knows of my arrest. They are fighting for me.*

I returned to my cell, and for the first time in eleven days, my mind and my body were finally able to relax.

I I I I I I

Mr. Sláma warned me that my release would likely take three months, but as New Year's Eve approached, rumors began to spread throughout the prison that the NISS would soon be releasing prisoners in honor of the upcoming sixtieth anniversary of Sudan's independence. According to the rumors, foreigners would be released first, followed by men accused of minor crimes.

On the evening of December 23, I heard a guard unlocking the door to my cell. A surge of adrenaline swept over me, and I couldn't help but feel hopeful.

Is this it? Am I going home?

I waited for the door to open, and to my great disappointment, I saw a new prisoner standing in the corridor. I felt dismayed and discouraged, realizing I was not about to be released. The man scanned the room, and his eyes settled on me. I quickly realized that the dynamics in my cell were about to change.

Abd al Bari stood no more than five feet tall and appeared to weigh at least four hundred pounds. He had cold eyes, dark hair, and a beard, and he spoke very good English with a perfect British accent. As he settled into our cell, I learned about his background. He was an arms dealer and weapons smuggler who grew up in Saudi Arabia before attending university in the United Kingdom. He'd been arrested in Khartoum on the suspicion that he was the head of a weapons-smuggling gang, and he prided himself on supplying weapons to ISIS fighters in Europe. He purchased machine guns for two hundred dollars apiece in South Sudan and resold them in the UK for five thousand pounds. This lucrative business led him to leave his successful IT business in the UK and dedicate his life to supplying the ISIS fighters in Europe.

At first, he was friendly to me, asking me my name and all about the circumstances of my arrest. But his facial expressions, overt friendliness, and general mannerisms gave me reason to suspect he had a more sinister agenda.

I soon heard from another cellmate that Abd al Bari had asked for special permission to be transferred to my cell.

| | | | | | |

On the morning of December 24, I woke up at 3:00 a.m. with my hand in a puddle of water. My blanket and clothes were wet.

I knew that there was no running water in my cell, so at some point in the night, a pipe must have burst. I looked around to see standing water covering the entire floor of the cell.

I had become so excited by the prospect of an imminent release from prison that, now, with my hopes shattered and my family far away, I started to cry and began complaining silently to the Lord.

Just then, in a moment that I will never forget, I clearly saw the face of Danjuma.

On January 28, 2015, Islamic radicals raided the small Christian village of Nunkwo in war-torn northern Nigeria. A thirteen-year-old boy named Danjuma Shakara was in the village when the attack began. He was a typical Nigerian boy who lived with his mother, a widow, and enjoyed fishing and playing with his friends.

However, at 6:00 a.m. on a Wednesday morning, Danjuma's life changed forever. He awoke to the sound of gunfire as more than one thousand armed extremists, disguised as herdsmen and backed by Boko Haram, infiltrated his village and began burning homes and killing the Christian inhabitants. Danjuma ran for his life, but he could not escape the machete-wielding insurgents who sliced his face, tore out his right eye, hacked at his left arm, and cut off his genitals.

The terrifying brutality left twenty-three people dead and thirty-eight injured. Danjuma's wounds were so horrific that the villagers walked by his mutilated body and assumed he was dead. They even dug a grave for him. Somehow, though, Danjuma survived. He regained consciousness and began crying and shouting. Villagers rushed him to the nearest city, some fifteen miles away, where he received medical treatment.

Three months later, after having been maimed and blinded, Danjuma could not conceal his beaming smile. The young Christian harbored no hatred for his attackers. "I forgive them," he had said, "because they don't know what they are doing."

After multiple surgeries and with the help of VOM, Danjuma returned to his mother's house with a life that looked very different than before. A permanent catheter extended out of his lower abdomen to drain his urine into a bag, which he carried with him. But instead of dying in the attack, Danjuma lived to tell others about Jesus. His grave, like that of his Savior, was still empty.

As I stood in my flooded cell, I saw Danjuma, and he was smiling. His spirit was like that. When I thought about him and the atrocities he experienced, I felt ashamed of the unexpressed complaints deep in my soul. Sooner or later, I would go home. I would continue to live my comfortable life, but Danjuma might not be able to see again until his death and resurrection. From that moment on, I began to pray for him every day.

| | | | | | |

My cellmates and I spent Christmas Eve cleaning our room and trying to dry our belongings. I welcomed the distraction because it gave me something to think about other than my family back home in the Czech Republic celebrating Christmas—the most anticipated day of worship in the Christian year. Thinking about my family celebrating the birth of Christ without me made me feel helpless and alone. This was the first Christmas I had ever been separated from my wife and children. As we worked, I remembered Christmas songs in my mind, songs my father taught me when I was a young boy.

The internal melodies encouraged me for a while, but when they flooded me with memories of my family and brought me to the brink of tears, I swept them from my mind like the water saturating my cell.

11

Back home in the Czech Republic, my wife and children had begun to face the fact that they would need to figure out how to handle our finances without me. But now, something more pressing had captured Váva's attention. As she sat at our dining room table helping Vanda, Váva opened her Skype account on her laptop. Suddenly, she saw that I was online.

"Are you there?" she typed. Nobody responded, but Váva knew someone was able to see her message.

"Can I speak with my father?" she asked. Still, no response.

"He is my father. Can I speak with him?" she repeated.

Váva suspected that someone had logged into my Skype account and was watching her type; suddenly, there seemed to be electrical pinpricks on the back of her neck. If my captors could access my Skype account, what *other* information might they be able to get? She jumped from the table and grabbed my iPad, which she knew would give her automatic access to both my Skype account and personal email, and scrambled to change my password. Vanda looked on with concern, a worried frown furrowing her brows. Váva clicked the link to notify Skype of a forgotten password, and within seconds a link to reset the login information arrived in my email inbox.

My family was now monitoring my online account. Soon, an automatic notification message appeared in my email inbox. Someone was trying to change my Skype password a second time, and this time the message was *in Arabic!*

| | | | | | | | |

Most of the guards at the NISS prison were afraid of the ISIS inmates and granted them special privileges like visiting each other's cells. On New Year's Eve, as the prisoners were eagerly expecting President Bashir to grant amnesty to some of the non-political cases, a friendly atmosphere filled our cell as all of us contemplated the joy of being released for the New Year. Abd al Bari told me that his reason for being transferred to our cell was because of the celebratory spirit, but I still suspected he had ulterior motives.

Abd al Bari had begun to harass me, and each day it intensified. When our morning tea arrived each day, he refused to pour more than an inch of the warm beverage into my dirty plastic cup. Not only did he physically limit my movement around the cell by cornering me and taking up space, forcing me into tight corners and intimidating me with his aggression and girth, but he also ordered me around. "When we are praying," he said, "you can't stand here. You have to be there."

When making me stand in the corner no longer satisfied him, he told me to remain perfectly motionless during their prayers and not look out the small window in the cell door. "You can't even stand here," he said. "You go to the toilet." My cellmates considered Abd al Bari the boss, and they made sure I obeyed his instructions. I felt utterly alone and increasingly concerned about my safety.

Even at first, when he was friendly to me, I never told him why I was really in the country. I only mentioned that I had recently visited some friends in Ethiopia and that the Sudanese airport security had confiscated my phone, laptop, and camera.

Soon, though, I realized that Abd al Bari had communicated my words to the interrogator, and in doing so, he had revealed his true reasons for requesting transfer to my cell: to glean information and to see me suffer.

| | | | | | |

One month earlier, just before I left home for Khartoum, Vanda and I visited my father, who was recovering from surgery to repair a broken leg at a hospital in Jindřichův Hradec, a city on the Czech Republic's southern border with Austria. His body was weak, but his mind was razor sharp, even at the age of eighty-nine.

I told him I was leaving for Sudan. "Khartoum this time," I assured him, "not to the civil war in the South."

"I will pray for you," he said with labored breath.

It was now the first week of January, and in my cell, I fell into a fitful sleep. I dreamed of the house where my father lived. I saw my sister working hard in the kitchen to prepare food for extended family members who had gathered. *Is the Lord sending me another message?*

When I woke from my sleep, I was certain of two things: I did not see my father, and the last time our extended family had come together was for a funeral.

12

By the first week of January 2016, I expected the NISS would have transferred my case to a court. I had been anticipating this date since my meeting with Mr. Sláma. January 10 would mark one month since my arrest. If my case was not transferred to a court by then, I knew this meant I would be released.

However, as the first week of January came and went, I soon realized that the NISS's interrogator had deliberately misled me with false information—it was a familiar tactic to me, one that I recognized from persecution under Communism. I felt frustrated and powerless. When the Czech consular officer failed to reappear with good news by January 9, I grew increasingly more agitated. "I want to contact the embassy," I told the guards. "I want to call my family." When they refused, I resolved to take things into my own hands. I began a hunger strike.

I was inspired by the memory of one of my coworkers, an Australian citizen who, when he was arrested in North Korea, began his own hunger strike. Because he was an elderly man, quickly deteriorating in the absence of nourishment, the North Koreans decided to release him. *If a hunger strike worked for him, perhaps it will work for me. If I have enough strength to succeed, maybe the Sudanese will release me as well.*

In Sudan, a hunger strike was considered a criminal act, and I understood the seriousness of my decision. Under Sudanese law, a prisoner undergoing a hunger strike could be tied to a pole in the courtyard with a bowl of food and cup of water placed near him. If he still refused to break his fast, he could be taken to court and charged for deteriorating his body. But I was determined, and I remembered my father's own forty-day spiritual fast years earlier. If he could subsist on water alone, then so could I.

Thankfully, my guards never resorted to legal action against me, and for eight days, I did not eat any food. I refused the bread and tea that the guards brought in the morning and the *fuhl*, or boiled beans, that they brought at 11:00. Not even boiled potatoes and pumpkin in the afternoon stew called *gara* could tempt me. It was easier to decline the evening meal, a bowl of noodles called *sheria*, because the sweet dish was often moldy. Instead, I only drank water and swallowed the aspirin-based headache relief that the guards delivered to my cell; on an empty stomach, I wondered if it would give me an ulcer. My commitment seemed to impress my ISIS cellmates, who equated my strike with their religious fasting during Ramadan even though their fasting from food and drink was only from dawn to dusk, followed by an entire night of gluttony.

By January 13, four days into my strike, I was in terrible shape. My trousers, which were already loose, stayed on my hips only with the help of a belt I'd fashioned from plastic bread bags. Neither my mind nor my body seemed to have any energy, and I lay on the floor motionless. The songs I once knew well were beginning to disappear from my mind. I could remember only vague snippets, but I lifted them up to the Lord anyway, the weak offerings of a man on the brink of collapse.

The guards transported me to the NISS hospital, where the medical staff performed a bevy of tests. In the month that I had been imprisoned, I had lost thirty-three pounds. The doctor was very kind and showed me the results of my blood count, and I was shocked at how low my hemoglobin level was. I had anemia, and whether the iron deficiency was from malnutrition or internal bleeding, I wasn't sure. But with twenty years of experience in this exact specialty—analytical chemistry, hematology, and blood transfusions—I knew the significance of my lab results. Ignoring my protests, the doctor ordered an infusion of dextrose in order to raise my blood glucose level, and it had the unintended result of giving me enough energy to continue my hunger strike for four more days.

I returned to the prison, but my low hemoglobin level was never far from my mind. I knew that the oxygen saturation of my blood was low, which in turn affected my brain, and given my tremendous difficulty concentrating, this made sense to me.

I felt trapped in the claustrophobic cell, surrounded constantly by incessant Muslim prayers and Arabic recitations of the Koran. By this time, I had memorized so much Arabic that I could be the muezzin or an imam. Even though I was constantly dizzy and struggled to concentrate, the Arabic words swirled around in my head. I worried constantly about my family, about how they would be able to make ends meet. I even struggled to formulate my own prayers. If I wasn't careful, I knew I could lose my mind.

On January 17, I was concerned enough about my health to stop my hunger strike. I stopped trying to take control of my own situation and instead gave everything in my life—including the duration of my time in prison—back to the Lord. It had been eight days since I last ate. The next morning, to help increase my weight and stamina, the guards began supplementing my breakfast with two small, plain yogurts and two boiled eggs.

I I I I I I

Allahu Akbar became a near-constant sound in the prison cell. It's part of the Muslim call to prayer, and each man repeated it incessantly over the course of the day, one hundred times each time they prayed. Confined in the tiny room, I watched my cellmates bow and listen to the words from the Koran. In the midst of all the murmuring voices and repetitious prayers, I started to worry about my mental health and felt a strong need for something besides their voices to occupy my mind.

In the final days of January, as my Muslim cellmates were praying, the Lord began to give me songs. Watching the Muslims bow their faces to the ground triggered the memory of a hymn that my father taught me when I was a little child: "Every Knee Shall Bow." During our underground church discipleship meetings in Czechoslovakia, we sang the hymn spontaneously and often, and in my prison cell, those same words began to rush into my mind. As the Muslims prayed, I sang the song in my mind, over and over, and it helped me to exalt the name of my Lord. Five times each day, as I stood near the bathroom of the cell to face the toilet, I remembered the refrain: "Every knee shall bow, every tongue confess that You are the Lord." By reminding myself that one day, every person's knees will bow before *my* Lord, I began to internalize the eternal reality of my victory in Christ, and my sanity stayed intact. In moments when I was most worried about my mental health, the Holy Spirit reminded me of Philippians 4:7: "And the peace of God, which surpasses all understanding, will guard your hearts and your minds in Christ Jesus." He was guarding not only my heart but also my mind.

During each call for prayer, as my cellmates washed themselves with water from the *ibrig*, I systematically praised God with words taken from Revelation 4:8: "The four living creatures ... day and night they never cease to say: 'Holy, holy, holy, is the Lord God Almighty, who was and is and is to come!'" If those four living creatures could say the words "holy, holy, holy" throughout eternity, then I knew I could manage to say them for one minute, for five minutes, or for an hour. I began repeating that verse over and over in my mind: "Holy, holy, holy, is the Lord God Almighty!"

Those words made me think of God's specific attributes—His holiness, His purity, His ability to heal. "Holy, holy, holy is God the healer." I began praying for the healing of the persecuted Christians in Nigeria who had recently been injured during a series of attacks. "Holy, holy, holy is God who sets the captives free." I prayed for the Christians in Eritrea, some of whom had been imprisoned for over a decade. "Holy, holy, holy is the Lord," I repeated to myself over and over again. I knew I couldn't sing my hymns aloud or speak the words of Scripture with my voice, but I could surely sing and say them in my heart.

When I began to focus more on the holiness and power of God and less on the horrors of my own situation, the dynamics in my prison cell began to change for the worse. My ISIS cellmates did not know that I had begun silently repeating these worshipful words, but during the first week of February, the more I sang to God and exalted His name, the more harshly they treated me. Since I was the only white man in the prison, my skin had become a particularly fruitful and constant source of ridicule. "Look how dirty your feet are," they sneered, pointing to my pale soles, "and look how clean our feet are."

My cellmates had become so aggressive that restricting my movement in the room no longer brought them any pleasure. Whenever I was walking, they made me stop to wait until they passed by. My cellmates forced me to sit cross-legged on the floor for hours at a time—a painful position since I was unaccustomed to the Muslim practice.

They also forced me to wash their underwear and scrub the toilet with my bare hands, leaving me feeling humiliated and degraded. Nor did they let me eat communally with them. "You are an infidel," they reminded me. They forced me to eat from a separate dish they stored near the toilet. Each time one of my cellmates relieved his bladder, my dish was splattered with urine droplets.

They called me all sorts of derogatory names, and when I failed to immediately answer to "filthy pig" or "filthy rat," they unscrewed the wooden handle of the broom from the floor and beat me over the head with it. Each morning, I woke with fresh bruises on my body and a throbbing headache.

So far, the Lord had given me the strength not to retaliate as they beat me. When they struck my right cheek, I offered them my left one. Of course, even if I chose to fight back and tried to defend myself against their assaults, my efforts would be fruitless against six men. There was no way I could fend them off, so I learned that if I wanted to stay alive, I needed to answer to whatever names they assigned me.

The Lord gave me a special grace not only to share the Gospel with them but also to live the Gospel among them. I knew it was not my old self but that it was Christ in me who enabled me to do that. When my cellmates saw that I consistently refused to retaliate against their attacks, their hatred and aggression grew even stronger. But I knew that we, as Christians, are supposed to love our enemies, to do good to those who hate us, to bless those who curse us, and to pray for those who abuse us (Luke 6:27). In fact, Christianity is the only religion that teaches its followers to love their enemies.

During the process of being admitted to the NISS prison, I had managed to keep my wedding ring because, as I was carrying more body weight, it wouldn't come off my finger. But as I continued to lose body mass in the cell, my finger had grown thin. I began to notice my cellmates looking at it.

"You have to give us the ring," they said. "If you don't give us this, we will kill you." I sometimes saw them sharpening the edge of one of the metal dishes and grinding down the blade of the air conditioner to use as knives.

One of my cellmates was a Libyan who said he used to serve as a personal bodyguard for Osama bin Laden. He showed his leg to us once, and it was peppered with scars from bullet holes. He also showed us how to kill a man from behind using the fishing line he'd smuggled into the prison. If done correctly, he explained, pulling the string from his pocket, death would come within a few seconds. The ISIS fighter bragged that he was among those who had beheaded twenty-one Egyptian Christians on the Libyan shore in February 2015, a videotaped execution that had been viewed all over the world. "I could kill anyone in seconds," he told me, winding the fishing line around his hands almost mindlessly. "If you were a Russian or an American, I would kill you on the spot."

My ISIS cellmates considered him a hero, and seeing him envy my wedding ring left me unnerved and feeling vulnerable. I knew that if he wanted to, this man could steal my ring—and my finger—in a second. I clenched my fingers around the thick band of gold, my only tangible connection to my precious wife at home.

I was forced to sit on the floor with my legs crossed as my cellmates pretended to be a team of interrogators questioning me about my Christian activity in Sudan. Whenever I gave them an answer they didn't like, they pummeled me with their fists. "Tell us what you are!" they screamed. "Tell us you are a filthy pig!"

Suddenly, their interrogation took an even more frightening turn. Abd al Bari forced me to my knees and began to beat me with the end of the broom handle—the only tool the guards permitted us to have in the cell. Each lash sent shocks of excruciating pain through my torso, and I gritted my teeth under his blows.

"Who are the other Christians who were arrested with you?" Abd al Bari demanded, pausing his blows. With my head still tucked against my chest, I felt my heart skip a beat. *What is he talking about? What other Christians?* I wondered. Another swift strike on my back, and then he rephrased his question. "How do you know Hassan and Monim?"

I was stunned. *Have they been arrested as well?* My body ached, and my mind raced as I tried to make sense of this information. I could feel my heartbeat in the contusions on my back, but these physical wounds weren't as painful as my next thought: *Have Hassan and Monim been arrested because of me?*

When I refused to answer questions about Pastor Hassan, the men smashed my fingers with the wooden stick. When I wouldn't give them names of other pastors at the conference in Addis Ababa, they slammed the heavy toilet door onto my elbow. A sharp, inhuman cry escaped from my lips as my brain tried to process the pain.

Sometimes, I was beaten so mercilessly that I didn't think I would survive another day. During his next interrogation, Abd al Bari kicked me so hard in my back with his shoe that I wondered if my rib had cracked. Not a day went by that I was not assaulted and tormented by my ISIS cellmates.

Surprisingly, as my torture increased, my mind grew more and more calm. No longer was I worried about my family at home or my Sudanese brothers imprisoned with me. In fact, during this season of physical suffering, I could not think of my family at all. I placed them on the altar and could only exalt the name of Jesus over them.

Through these experiences, horrific as they were, I was beginning to see a clearer picture of Jesus Christ who was also beaten and bruised. Each time I was slapped, punched, kicked, or ridiculed, I thought of Christ and what He patiently endured at the hands of the Roman soldiers.

If my Lord was willing to endure punishment for me, then as His follower, I must be willing to walk in His steps and to share the sufferings for His name's sake (Philippians 3:10).

I I I I I I

Each evening, my ISIS cellmates continued their interrogation. Specifically, Abd al Bari wanted to know more about the Christian work in Sudan. Most of my answers they did not like, so they continued to hit me with the wooden handle of the broomstick in our cell. They beat my head and my fingers, and they jabbed the end into my stomach. My body writhed with pain, but to my great surprise, I realized that I felt a deep peace in my heart and mind. I was even able to pray for my family as they beat me.

Suddenly, for a fraction of a second, I saw Christ before my eyes as the Jewish religious police beat Him on His head with a wooden stick after His arrest in Matthew 27:30. "Lord," I prayed, "you went this way ahead of me and were beaten, crucified, and even died for my sins." At once, I made a startling realization: I was aware that I was being ruthlessly beaten by my ISIS cellmates, but I did not feel the pain!

I knew the Lord was with me in the cell. I would later find out that God had called forth an army of prayer warriors on my behalf—right at that very moment. But I didn't know that then.

| | | | | | |

One day, I was sitting in my cell listening to the members of ISIS talk about how my country, the Czech Republic, allowed the United States' CIA to torture al-Qaeda terrorists with waterboarding. I recognized that my cellmates had confused my country with Poland, so I corrected their narrative.

They insisted that it was my country, though, not Poland, that allowed the US to waterboard the terrorists. "Do you know what waterboarding is?" they asked me.

"Yes," I said, "I know what waterboarding is."

"Okay, but you don't know how it feels, so we are going to show you." At first, I was not concerned. Our cell had little running water, so I knew these were empty threats.

However, I soon realized how serious they were. Abd al Bari convinced the guards to transfer all of us to a larger room on our floor, one the prisoners called the "water room" because it was the only room in the prison with consistent water pressure.

On the morning of February 6, all seven of us were transferred to our new cell, and my cellmates forced me to wash their underwear in the corner where the filthy toilet was. With my back turned, I heard the six men talking about me in Arabic, and I began to grow worried. Osama Ramadan, a man I had overheard praying at night a few weeks earlier, apparently would be spearheading the waterboarding. I saw him folding strips of cloth that had been cut from a *jilahbiyah*, one of the Muslims' long robes. "You should tell the interrogator what we are doing to you," the men taunted. Even from prison, nothing could stop them from fighting the infidels.

In my physical condition, I knew that being waterboarded might end my life. Not only was I weak from repeated beatings, but I also suspected that I continued to battle anemia and hypoxia. As the men walked toward me, I took a few seconds to calm my heart and prepare my mind for whatever horrors would happen next.

13

At noon on February 6, as my ISIS-sympathizing cellmates were finalizing their torture preparations, a man they called "Mean Guard" for his refusal to acquiesce to their demands stood just outside the cell and listened. His keys jingled in his hand. Mean Guard quickly figured out what was going on inside the room and, despite having never shown any care for me before, burst into the cell.

In a stream of angry Arabic, he ordered me to gather my belongings and go with him. I left the pile of unwashed clothes on the floor, and as I followed Mean Guard out of the cell, I turned to see the shocked and disappointed faces of my cellmates. This must have been how Daniel felt when he was taken out from the lions' den.

I spent one night in another cell with two Muslims, secular businessmen. This cell was slightly smaller but even dirtier than my other one. On the first day, I helped them clean our dirty cell, so they sympathetically shared their food with me. When they saw my wounds—the black and blue bruises on my head, elbows, and back, they were shocked. So I told them what happened to me when I was still with the men from ISIS.

The next evening, I was called downstairs for yet another interrogation in the NISS prison. The air conditioning was blowing on me, and I immediately felt chilled. In the center of the small room was a table with two people sitting in chairs. I knew the routine. One of the men would play "good cop," and the other would be harsher. I examined the interrogation officer. He was dressed nicely in a jacket and tie and smelled of cologne—a fragrance that I had become accustomed to smelling in Sudan where it was applied more heavily than in Europe or America. I sat in the chair designated for me and glanced at the shelf on the table that contained drawers of documents. I felt curious about the interrogation, wondering why they had summoned me. From the Sudanese Security interrogator, I finally learned that my father had, in fact, passed away. It had been more than a month since his death, and even though God had already prepared me to receive the news through my dream, this confirmation felt like a punch to my stomach. I wondered how my family was coping with the loss. My mind wandered back to the Czech Republic, back to my family. More than anything, I wanted to be there to support them through this difficult season of mourning. My mind also retrieved a memory that filled me with resolve for this interrogation and for however long my imprisonment might last.

My mind went back to my first year of high school. My parents had organized a youth discipleship meeting at our house. We had as many as fifty people come and stay in our four-bedroom house for a couple of days. Boys slept in one room, girls in another.

When the meeting ended and everyone safely returned home, all of us breathed a sigh of relief. The police had not discovered us; the meeting had not been raided. We thanked God that everything had gone without any trouble.

My school was only five hundred yards from our house, so I walked back and forth each day. One day, about two weeks after the youth gathering, I arrived home to discover that no one was there. This wasn't completely unusual; my siblings were older than I was, and all three of them had moved out for jobs or university. My mother was a kindergarten teacher, and the only school where she could find a job after people found out she was a Christian was about a thirty-minute train ride from our home. She could have taught at a school closer to our home, but she refused to sign "the pledge" to raise up all of her students to follow the great ideals of the atheistic Communist Party. Most afternoons, I would meet her at the train station, and we'd walk home together.

When I had been home for an hour, and then two, without anyone else arriving, I began to worry. Had something happened to my parents? Had the police discovered the youth meeting we'd hosted in our home? Had they been arrested? Should I call one of the other leaders and warn them?

I was growing more and more fearful when my dad arrived home late that evening. My mom arrived a little while later. I rushed to hug them both, feeling the tension that had built up in my mind and heart relax.

As we sat at the dinner table that night, my parents compared notes about their day. My father had been approached by two uniformed policemen and "invited" to go with them to the local police station.

For my mother, the treatment had been more humiliating. Two uniformed policemen and two secret police had gone into her classroom and escorted her out in front of her students. She was pleased that she'd been able to place a phone call to her husband. "They picked me up," she whispered. "Me too," my dad replied before the call was cut off.

My parents always knew this was a possibility. It was part of following Christ in a Communist country, and they had counted the cost early on in their walk of faith. I will never forget that dinner-table conversation as my parents discussed their interrogations, comparing notes on the questions they'd been asked and the ways they had answered them. They specifically recalled ways that the interrogators had tried to trip them up and discussed the best ways to answer those questions in the future. At the time, the conversation was shocking to me. What families sit around at dinner and discuss how to handle being interrogated by the secret police? Little did I know, that dinner-table conversation was preparing me to someday sit in the room I was in now.

Later that night, my father handed me a book. It would become the second-most important book in my life after the Bible. One of my father's colleagues had brought a German-language copy of Richard Wurmbrand's book *In God's Underground* from some of the Christian brothers in Germany. Even today, I can clearly remember my father handing it to me and saying, "You need to read this book." Since I was fluent in German, I read it cover to cover, stopping all other activities. Richard's testimony deeply moved me at the time.

And now, many years later, as I sat and listened to this interrogator tell me about my father's death, I thought yet again about the terrible torture Richard had to endure and realized that my situation paled in comparison to his. The interrogator then asked me how I was doing in prison.

"Now, I am doing better," I said, "because they moved me to another cell."

"What happened for them to move you?"

With a voice shaking with pent-up emotion, I told him about the beatings, the torture, the waterboarding. Enraged, he pulled out his cell phone and made a call. I could understand most of the long conversation in Arabic. He had called the prison commander and was demanding to know how these things could have happened to me.

Then he hung up the phone and began asking me for information about myself—my initials, my full name, specific details that could only mean one thing: the NISS had finished their investigation, and I was about to be released.

By the time the interrogator finished his final meeting with me, it was very late. I was escorted back to my new cell on the fourth floor, where both of my cellmates were already asleep. With my blanket in hand, I found an open place on the floor and tried to rest.

Thoughts of my father consumed me, and I couldn't sleep. In fact, I couldn't even lie down. *Maybe I should stand up and walk.*

As memories from my childhood came to my mind, I was filled with thanksgiving to the Lord for my father's life. I had tears in my eyes, but they were not tears of sadness. Rather, they were tears of joy and thankfulness for the life I experienced growing up in a Christian family and the example of faithfulness that my father had lived out— even under persecution.

I knew I would see my father again one day, and I was absolutely sure of God's presence with me in the cell.

All of a sudden, a guard entered the room. "Beter," he said, pointing to my small plastic bag of clothes, and struggling, like the other Arab guards, to pronounce the "P" of my name, "bring your stuff and come with me." I felt somewhat excited, hoping that my release had finally arrived.

"The blanket as well?" I asked.

"No, no, leave the blanket here."

Finally, I knew I was being released! Why else wouldn't I need my blanket? In a matter of days, I'd be back in the Czech Republic with my family, sharing my testimony of God's faithfulness during my two months in prison. At night, I would share a warm bed with my wife.

I picked up my bag, and we left the room. I followed him down the corridor toward the elevator, but inexplicably, we stopped at the door to another cell. All of a sudden, I knew that I had been seriously mistaken. This was a room with a reputation—a room every man in the prison feared. I'd passed by it many times on my way to be interrogated, and now that I was standing at its door, I could feel my blood beginning to chill in my veins.

I had arrived at the "Refrigerator."

14

I stepped into the empty room and immediately heard the flow of the cold air rushing in. There was a metal bed without a mattress, and it was covered with dried human blood. The toilet was filthy, and the Refrigerator had no running water. I thought of my blanket and estimated that the temperature in my new cell was approximately fifty degrees Fahrenheit. *This is going to be a cold night.*

It dawned on me that my transfer to the Refrigerator was likely an act of revenge on the part of the guards whom the prison commander had reprimanded for my mistreatment. I tensed up, realizing they were now going to show me that they were the masters here.

After this long in prison, short grey hair had begun to cover my head, but there wasn't much of it, so I wrapped my extra shirt around my head like a hat. I dug again into the plastic bag and removed my extra pair of trousers. Without a jacket, I used them to cover my exposed arms.

All night, I walked. If I stopped moving, the cold felt unbearable. Once, I tried to rest on the room's lone chair, but the metal against my legs made me colder.

In the midst of my discomfort, though, there was a hidden blessing: for the first time since I arrived at the prison, I was alone. *I could speak out loud!* I praised the Lord for my father and wondered if God would surround me with angels, like he had during Richard Wurmbrand's imprisonment. As I thought about Richard and his fourteen years in prison, a strange thing happened.

An odd sensation, like someone wrapping me from behind in a pre-warmed coat, covered my body, and the phrase "My Lord, my God" spilled spontaneously from my lips. It was the Lord who was keeping me warm. Though this solitary confinement was supposed to be a punishment, I felt that it was my first liberation inside the prison walls! For the first time in two months, I was able to pray out loud.

Throughout the night, I even tried to sing some Christian songs. When I was fifteen years old, I memorized the wonderful song "Thine Be the Glory," whose melody was written by Georg Friedrich Handel. I had tried to sing it while I was still with my ISIS cellmates, but I could never remember more than the first three or four words. But suddenly, there in solitary confinement, I experienced a miracle with my memory. The Holy Spirit instantly reminded me of the first two complete verses of this powerful song. I felt like a poet who receives a moment of inspiration and writes and writes until a beautiful, complete poem is written in only a few minutes. I received the words as I continued to sing out loud in faith. I was sure that the guards, along with all of the other prisoners, suspected that I had gone mad after only one single night in solitary confinement.

The next morning, the guards finally stopped the cold air and brought me my blanket. I sniffed the blanket and could smell the scent of another prisoner on it, and I knew someone else had used it during the night. Nevertheless, I was thrilled to have my blanket back.

By then, three weeks after my hunger strike ended, I was quite thirsty, but only a drip of water fell from the nearby faucet. I found a cup of yogurt in my plastic bag, left over from my breakfast supplement following the hunger strike. I ate the yogurt and used the cup to collect the water droplets. It took at least fifteen minutes, but finally the cup was full.

Step by step, the Lord showed me what to do next. First, I began my search for whatever was blocking the flow of water. The Lord guided me to the dark corner of the toilet where I found the main water shut-off valve. It was closed, and there was no handle with which I could open it. I kept searching through the rubbish on the floor for something that would allow me to open the valve. Finally, I found a piece of metal and made my way back toward the toilet. When I turned the valve with the piece of metal, water flowed freely into the lavatory, and the toilet bowl filled. Next, I found a small strip of cloth and dipped it into the water, which now flowed freely from the faucet. Using the wet cloth and my prison-issued carbolic soap, I disinfected my body.

Once my body was clean, I turned my attention to the room. It took an entire day, but I finally removed the blood stains from the bed. Eventually, I deemed the bed clean enough to drape with my blanket.

My transfer to the solitary cell became, to me, a type of partial freedom. The ISIS men were always afraid of being placed in solitary confinement and knew that if a prisoner was there longer than a week, he would lose his mind. For that reason, the guards, who bowed in fear to the wishes of the imprisoned militants, never held the ISIS fighters in solitary for more than two or three days.

For me, though, solitary confinement was the time when my memory returned. I remembered the songs that we used to sing during times of Communist persecution. I began to recall the Scripture verses that I memorized when I was young. All of this came back to me at exactly the right time, just when I needed it the most. On the third day, the Holy Spirit gave me the final verse to "Thine Be the Glory." It usually took at least a week or two per song, but eventually, I was able to remember all the words to many, many more hymns.

Thankfully, the cold blasts of air in the Refrigerator did not return.

In order to regain my strength, I spent my days walking, beginning at 6:00 a.m. and not stopping until at least 9:00 at night.

I calculated that I covered approximately fifteen miles each day, and while I walked, I prayed.

This experience of communion with God amazed me. Like Richard Wurmbrand, I, too, felt the immediacy of His presence, the closeness and intimacy of His healing power. For a month and a half, from February 7 until March 29, I shared my cell with only the Lord.

Of course, not every morning was bright and joyful. Often, a great sadness flooded my heart and mind. I tried to sleep during the day, but the sadness became even heavier when lying horizontally, so I immediately jumped up and continued my morning prayer walk. There were days when I had to proclaim, "The Lord Jesus is my peace! The Lord Jesus is my joy!" In the midst of my overwhelming sadness, I repeated these words for several minutes while walking around my cell until those truths became my reality.

| | | | | | |

On the morning of Monday, February 22, 2016, the prison guards arrived at my solitary cell and ushered me downstairs. There, I discovered that I had received a surprise visit from the NISS interrogating officer.

"You need to shave your face," he said, frowning at my long beard.

"It's not so easy to do that here," I explained. He looked down at my slippered feet and handed me my shoes from the prison storage room.

"Put on better clothes," he said. I refused because all of my clothes were similar in style, and besides, I knew the ones I was wearing were clean because I'd been washing them regularly. *Why would it matter what I wear?* I was baffled by this sudden attention to my appearance. *Is someone from the Czech government coming to visit Sudan? Why else would it matter what I look like?* Then, I entertained a thought almost too good to be true: *Is it possible I am about to be released?*

The prison guards cuffed my hands with heavy, painful chains and led me outside to a van. Six heavily armed officers climbed into the van after me. This was a routine I had done once before, on the day I met Mr. Sláma at the National Club. But this time, there was an uncomfortable change in procedure. So that I could not see the street names of our route, one of the guards covered my head with a thick, black hood. I began to panic as I realized that the hood prevented me from breathing properly.

When the van slowed to stop and the guard next to me finally removed the black hood, I was relieved to see that we were once again at the National Club. As we waited in the van, I noticed a black Mercedes pulling into our parking lot. The car stopped, and four men exited—two Sudanese security guards and two white men who didn't appear to be Sudanese and might even have been Czech.

"Do you know them?" one of my guards asked.

"No."

As soon as the four men entered the National Club, I was escorted into the building and shown to the room where they were waiting. They didn't introduce themselves to me but announced that they were from the Czech Intelligence Service. What followed was a series of odd questions.

"Are you in touch with any foreign intelligence?" they asked.

"No, I'm not," I said.

"Are you in touch with any military intelligence?"

"I completed one year of compulsory military service under Communism, but no, nothing else."

Soon, our meeting drew to a close, and I received devastating news: The Sudanese government would not be releasing me. Instead, my case would, in fact, go to the Sudanese court. The disappointment nearly overwhelmed me. I left the National Club feeling dejected and depressed, and slowly I understood all the fuss over my clothes and shoes. The NISS interrogation officer wanted me to receive a clear message: the only serious partner with which they would negotiate is the intelligence service—not diplomats, not the consular office, and not even the ambassador herself.

| | | | | | |

At some point in mid-February, the international media learned of my arrest. My photo appeared on the Interpol website, listing me as a missing person in Khartoum. Then, on Saturday, February 27, 2016, as I walked around my solitary cell in the NISS prison, my wife walked into a local gas station outside of Prague. Not having had any other contact with me, her eyes came to rest on a stack of newspapers near the door—the weekend edition of *DNES*, the daily newspaper of the Czech Republic.

Her heart nearly stopped when she read the headline: "The Czech Held in Sudan Is Threatened with the Death Penalty." Unable to quell the tears rising in her eyes, Vanda bought the paper and rushed to her car to begin the fast-paced journey home to tell our children the terrible news.

15

A week and a half after I was moved to solitary confinement, at about the time my photo appeared on the Interpol website, Mr. Sláma, the consular officer from the Czech Embassy, was able to travel from Egypt to meet with me again. With a shaking voice and tears in my eyes, I told him of the torture I had experienced, first at the hands of my ISIS cellmates and then in my freezing cell.

"Please do not tell this to my family," I urged him, "because they would worry about me even more." Mr. Sláma seemed to understand and nodded in agreement. When I returned to my cell after our meeting, I once more heard the quiet hiss of flowing air, and a freezing chill again filled the room. Instantly, I knew that the return of the cold air was an act of revenge: the NISS officers were punishing me for telling Mr. Sláma about my torture.

On his next visit, on March 10, 2016, he brought me a welcome surprise—two letters from my family back home in the Czech Republic along with a supplement they had sent in order to help with my anemia. My adrenaline surged as I felt my heart begin beating violently in my chest. As quickly as I could, I ripped open the letters. It had been so long since I had corresponded with my family. Never had I been this desperate to hear how they were doing.

According to the NISS guidelines, the letters had to be written in English, so Váva served as the family scribe. As I began reading the first letter, dated February 1, tears came to my eyes. "We hope this letter finds you in good health," my daughter wrote, "and that you are being well looked after. You know that we miss you very much and are patiently waiting for you to be home soon." Váva was in good health, and my wife was returning to work after recovering from a recent episode of the flu. Everything inside me became warm as I read that "she misses you very much and thinks about you a lot."

My daughter had just passed her final exam in Internal Medicine. The next week, if she passed her final exam in Gynecology and Obstetrics, she hoped to apply for work at the hospital. A smile spread across my face as I learned that my son, Petr, was also studying diligently for his final exam on February 3. After passing it, he would begin preparing for his bachelor's thesis. I felt so proud of my children. If only I could have been with them. But then, as I glanced down the page, I read a paragraph that made my heart sink into my stomach.

"We are really sorry to tell you," my daughter wrote, "that your father passed away at the beginning of January. He was able to spend Christmas at home with family, but just after Christmas, his health deteriorated. He had to be transported to the hospital again, and he passed away quietly after a few days, which was on the 4th of January." The mention of my father's death hit me afresh, and I felt exasperated, once more, that he had died weeks before the NISS interrogator bothered to tell me the news.

I continued reading the letter and discovered that all the household affairs were being taken care of. My mother-in-law was staying with my family during this time, and even though she was heartbroken by my imprisonment, her health continued to improve. My brother seemed to be accepting our father's death also, but I knew that he must have been struggling since he had been my father's main caregiver.

My eyes lingered for a few seconds and then scrolled down the page. My family had been in contact with the Czech Ministry of Foreign Affairs and also with Mr. Sláma. The end of the letter came too quickly and tugged hard at my heart. "We all miss you very much, and all the relatives and friends are thinking about you. With love, Vanda, Váva, and Petr."

I put down the first letter and immediately read the next, which was dated February 16, two weeks later. "Dear Petr," it began. My hands were shaking as I brought the page to my face. "We are really glad that we were able to write you the previous letter and that you were able to read it. We hope that you are healthy and that there is no physical or psychological disability. We really miss you, and we think about you all the time. Mother is sad that you are not at home, but we all believe that we will find out about each other soon."

Through Váva, Vanda explained that my children were suffering greatly from the absence of their grandfather, and my brother was experiencing the deepest grief. I learned that my family had been in close contact with my sisters, and not only was my mother-in-law's health continuing to improve, but my wife was also fully recovered from her illness and was planning a trip to visit her cousin, Jana. My daughter passed her final exam in Gynecology and Obstetrics and even received the highest grade possible, an "A." And after taking a few days off to care for the family and assist with housework, she was hard at work studying for her final exam in Pediatrics. I was confident she would pass. My son, having also passed his last exam without any problems, finished his semester successfully. I was glad to know that my family was still in contact with the Ministry of Foreign Affairs and the Czech Embassy in Cairo, and I savored the last few lines of the letter for as long as I could: "Everybody who knows you is intensively thinking about you."

During this visit, I was finally allowed to write my first letter from prison. I'd dreamed of this moment for so long, composing the letter in my mind and thinking constantly about what I would include. I could hardly believe the opportunity had finally arrived. There was so much I was eager to tell them—months of thoughts and prayers, emotions and encouragements, comforts and explanations. But with the consular officer sitting on one side of me and an interrogator on the other, I was permitted only a few seconds to write the letter, and I could write only in English. My mind raced, and I thought quickly, knowing that I needed to be careful with my words. In hurried capital letters, I scribbled the note to Vanda:

My Dear,

This is just a short greeting from Sudan to let you know I am OK. Thanks for your two letters that I was able to read in the presence of the Czech Republic representatives. I am doing well, praying for you all. I know that the whole case is in the Lord's hands. I am doing well, and I am glad that you are doing well too. Looking forward to coming home soon.

God bless you all.
Petr

The interrogator took a photo of the correspondence for his records and then handed it to Mr. Sláma. The consular officer folded my letter and slipped it into his briefcase. "I will see you again on April eighth," he said, and then he left.

| | | | | | |

Even one or two days in the Refrigerator is enough to drive a prisoner mad. But to the great surprise of the guards, I was still sane, even after weeks in solitary confinement and two long spells of unbearable cold. Unexpectedly, Mean Guard arrived at the Refrigerator one day, and I was deeply moved when I saw him. He had taken me from the lion's den just as I was about to be waterboarded, and with tears in my eyes, I thanked him for saving my life. I quietly told him my email address and invited him to stay in my home if he ever made it to Europe. He was moved as well, and tears streamed from his eyes, too.

Over the following weeks, we became close friends. Whenever he was on duty, he came by my solitary cell and gave me an extra portion of morning tea or evening food. Finally having a full cup of tea was an emotional moment for me, because fresh in my mind was the memory of the ISIS men giving me less than an inch of tea at the bottom of my dirty cup. The Lord reminded me of a verse from the Bible, Mark 9:41: "For truly, I say to you, whoever gives you a cup of water to drink because you belong to Christ will by no means lose his reward." As I sipped the warm beverage, I thanked the Lord for His kindness to me. Even in solitary confinement, He had given me the friendship of Mean Guard.

I   I   I   I   I   I

On March 29, two and a half weeks after I wrote my wife the letter, one of the NISS guards came into my cell. "Oh, you cleaned everything," he said with a friendly and appreciative tone. I had, in fact, cleaned the cell and toilet area so I could walk on the floor barefoot. "Petr, take all your stuff and come with me," he said. *I'm being released!*

I shoved my dirty prison clothes into my plastic bag. *Should I bring my blanket?* Even though I would not need it anymore, I decided to keep it as a memento. It was, after all, a gift from my kind cellmate and an early reminder of God's faithfulness to me here in prison.

As I walked down the corridor, I saw Pastor Hassan and my interpreter, Monim, watching me through the window in the door of a nearby cell. I had first learned of their arrest from my ISIS cellmates. They had "interrogated" me about my work and why I was in Sudan, and they told me that "my coworkers" had also been arrested. I learned later who those "coworkers" were. Through the window in my cell one day, I saw Pastor Hassan being led down the hall toward interrogation, and I prayed for him immediately.

Now, seeing Hassan and Monim's faces through the window in the door, I wondered when or even *if* I would ever see them again, and I silently prayed God would encourage, strengthen and protect my Sudanese brothers—hopeful that they, too, would soon be released.

The guard took me downstairs to the storage room, where he gave me back my carry-on suitcase. I opened it, and to my surprise, I saw all the medicine my family had been sending me. The guards had been hiding it this whole time, even the anemia medicine that I needed so desperately. I also saw in my suitcase the toilet paper, deodorant, and cologne that Mr. Sláma had been bringing me on each visit. This was the first I'd seen of them; the contents of the suitcase were a welcome sight.

I had gone four months without using a towel, shampoo, or even a razor blade to shave with. Only the carbolic soap and a few small bottles of water had kept my skin clean. When the guard left the storage room, I removed my dirty pants and T-shirt, placed them in the suitcase, and put on my clean clothes—clothes I hadn't seen or felt in nearly four months. I applied the deodorant and cologne, smiling at the thought of seeing Vanda again.

"Come with us," the guard said, allowing me to bring my suitcase. I sighed in relief as I thought about my release to come. *Finally!* Without even handcuffing me, he led me outside to a minibus to take me, hopefully, to the airport. It was 9:00 p.m., and I knew that Turkish Airlines had a flight leaving Khartoum around 1:00 a.m.

Within hours, I would again be a free man. *At last, I am going home!*

I looked out the window and saw planes taking off and landing at the airport. As our minibus approached the left turn to the entrance of the terminal, though, the driver didn't seem to be slowing. I darted my eyes in confusion toward him, but the man's eyes were fixed on the road ahead. *What is happening?* I flashed my eyes back toward the airport as we drove straight by without even slowing down. I watched as the airport disappeared behind me in the distance, feeling utterly crestfallen. A punch in the stomach would have been far less painful than this crushing disappointment. All my hopes of returning to my family grew smaller by the second, and they eventually vanished entirely as the road stretched out before me.

Several minutes later, we arrived at a building marked "Niyaba Mendola," the local Khartoum police station. The building was in a shocking state of disrepair—so dreadful that it made the NISS prison look like a palace by comparison.

They led me into a bustling office with a constant stream of policemen and NISS officers. In the small room, I saw my laptop bag resting on the table. A spark of hope reignited inside me. *They brought me to this security building to return all my belongings!* One of the men walked over to the table and reached into my laptop bag.

"Is this your computer?" he asked me, setting it on the table.

"Yes," I said, eagerly.

The man scribbled something onto a piece of paper, then grabbed my camera and other electronic devices. One by one, he asked me the same question about each piece of equipment and then checked them off the list. *This must be part of the exit documentation process.*

His next move, though, crushed my spirit yet again. Instead of putting the equipment back into the bag, he handed them to some of the other policemen in the room. "You will have a chance to compare which prison is the best," he said, smirking at me.

At that moment, I knew the guards had no intention of taking me to the airport. They placed me in an investigation room. A few minutes later, a man came in and announced, "You are now being transferred to us, and we will carefully prepare your case before it goes to court."

The general of security entered the room. I recognized his checkered jacket and remembered him interrogating me at the Khartoum airport. When he saw me wearing my clean clothes, he began to laugh. He looked at my confused face, and his laughs grew louder. Helplessly, I watched him enjoy the moment, powerless to do anything but wait. The guards' game—their attempt to trick me into thinking I'd be released—had been successful.

My father, a pastor, holding me when I was just two years old. My parents were frequently monitored and interrogated by the secret police in Communist Czechoslovakia because of their work in the unofficial church, which was not approved by the government.

I was fifteen years old when I received a copy of Richard Wurmbrand's book In God's Underground *in German. My father handed the book to me after he returned home from being interrogated by secret police. On that day, both of my parents were arrested at the same time in two different locations. They were not home after I had returned from school that day, and I wondered what had happened to them. When my father came home, he saw how scared I was, so he told me: "Read this book. It will encourage your faith."*

My father and me during my first leave from mandatory
military duty in Communist Czechoslovakia. During the
first month of my compulsory military service, I had a great
opportunity to confess my Christian faith before a large crowd
of soldiers. After being too ashamed to admit my father was
a pastor when I was in fourth grade, I had asked the Lord to
give me an opportunity to confess Christ before people. The
opportunity came during my military training, which assumed
an atheistic worldview, when an officer asked, "Is there anyone
who still believes in God?" In that moment, I clearly felt like,
"Petr, this is the time you can publicly confess Christ." So I raised
my hand. I was the only person among three hundred soldiers.
Since that time, I was always trying to witness for Christ.

Christians in Sudan have been persecuted under the leadership of former President Omar Hassan al-Bashir, who rose to power in 1989 through a military coup and established a strict form of Islamic law throughout the country. In March 2009, the Hague-based International Criminal Court issued a warrant for his arrest—the first warrant ever for a sitting head of state—charging him with committing war crimes and crimes against humanity, including mass extermination, deportation, torture, and rape. Bashir continued to lead Sudan until the Sudanese military ousted him as president on April 11, 2019, after several months of protests.

In December 2002, I traveled to Sudan a second time. On this trip, I accompanied a mission colleague and distributed practical help to persecuted Christians in the northern Upper Nile region, which at that time was approximately twelve miles from the frontline. I also encouraged Sudanese Christians, sharing from the Czech Bible that I had received when I was seven years old. This Bible was smuggled into Communist Czechoslovakia in the late 1960s. Having been on the receiving end of such help during Communist persecution, it was exciting for me to encourage my persecuted brothers and sisters in Sudan and distribute help to them.

I first met Aida Skripnikova in St. Petersburg, Russia, in December 2002. She had spent four years in prison in the 1960s because of her Christian outreach in the Soviet Union. Aida's remarkable story is told in the book Hearts of Fire.

In my work as The Voice of the Martyrs' Regional Director for Africa,
I visited a young boy named Weng in northern Nigeria. When Weng
was just three weeks old, Muslim extremists attacked his village.
They set his house on fire and killed his mother as she attempted
to flee with Weng in her arms. Weng fell into the fire, burning his
feet so badly that they were unable to develop normally. On this
trip, VOM provided Weng with new prostheses, which allowed him
to walk and run like other kids his age. Just three weeks after this
photo was taken, I traveled to Sudan, where I was arrested.

*I secretly wrote these notes while reading the Bible in prison,
especially while I was in solitary confinement for three months in
the Niyaba Mendola police station. During this time, I experienced
what I would call a private Bible study with the Holy Spirit.
Standing at my cell window from 8 a.m. until 5 p.m. every day,
I finished reading my Bible from Genesis to Revelation in three
weeks. For the first five months of my prison experience, I was not
allowed to have a Bible.*

This photo of me with (from left to right) Pastor Hassan, Pastor Kuwa, and Brother Monim was taken in the Al-Huda prison chapel. On January 29, Pastor Hassan and Brother Monim were each sentenced to twelve years in prison, while I was later sentenced to life in prison. Pastor Kuwa was acquitted on January 2, as he was not present in Khartoum during my visit. His arrest came as a result of his missionary outreach among Muslims in his country.

This is the first cup I received in prison for my morning tea. The cup was very dirty when it was given to me, and I did not have enough water to clean it properly. I could only clean it with the desert sand at Al-Huda prison. As my beard and hair grew very long, I desperately needed a comb. The comb in the photo was given to me by the Czech consular office. The Czech Bible I read in prison is open to Psalm 103, which is one of several sections of Scripture that I memorized, unsure of how long I would be able to keep the Bible with me.

Pastor Hassan (right), another elder from the prison chapel (left), and me at Al-Huda prison. When Pastor Hassan, Pastor Kuwa, and I arrived at Al-Huda prison, we were invited to the chapel on the first day. Having three more preachers, the elders decided to increase the number of services in the prison chapel from two a week to five per week. During my free time, I taught fellow prisoners French and English.

*On Christmas Eve, I preached in the
Al-Huda prison chapel to more than two
hundred prisoners. On Christmas Day,
prison authorities allowed about one
hundred prisoners who were on death row
to attend the service. There was a great
spiritual hunger among the prisoners.
When I first arrived at the Al-Huda
prison chapel, only twenty to twenty-five
attended. Nearly five months later, there
were more than two hundred people
attending this service. On Christmas Day,
a Catholic priest originally from Italy was
allowed to visit the prison chapel. Before
he started his sermon in Arabic, he said in
English that he had never preached before
so many people, not even in Rome.*

MLADÁ FRONTA   sobota 27. 2. a neděle 28. 2. 2016   18 Kč

DNES

STŘEDNÍ ČECHY

Čínská mise:
kraj hlásí splněno
Vyslanci S-čchuanu mají přivést
do kraje investory a turisty

Čechovi v Súdánu hrozí trest smrti

DiCaprio, nebo Stallone? Str. 12

MF DNES zjistila, proč Súdán už měsíce vězní českého občana. V přísně islámské zemi natáčel svědectví o pronásledování křesťanů.

Karel Hrubeš
reportér MF DNES

PRAHA, CHARTÚM Petra Jaška čeká brzy soud. Začít by mohl už do konce března.

MF DNES nyní zjistila konkrétní důvody, proč ho režim východoafrického Súdánu zavřel začátkem prosince do vězení.

Podle informací MF DNES je klíčovým důkazem proti dvaapadesátiletému muži videonahrávka, kterou během svého pobytu v rigidně islámské zemi pořídil. Na ní je výpověď popáleného muže, který popisuje, jak přišel ke zranění. Podle Jaška to bylo při násilnostech muslimů proti křesťanům. Jenže muž z videa svou výpověď před súdánskými úřady popřel a uvedl, že Jašek jeho slova vytrhl z kontextu. Zranění si prý přivodil při nehodě.

Jašek je navíc obviněn z nelegálního překročení státní hranice.

Tomu, že přijel do Súdánu pomáhat súdánským křesťanům, nasvědčuje, že jeho cestu hradila americká organizace Voice of Martyrs (Hlas mučedníků). Její pobočka s názvem Občanské hnutí Pomoc pronásledované církvi sídlí v Česku.

Čeští diplomaté, kteří se marně snažili vyjednat Jaškovo propuštění, si nejsou jisti, jaký trest hrozí. Podle informací MF DNES je však situace vážná.

Súdán má v ústavě zakotveny prvky tradičního islámského práva. Šaría a snahu o šíření křesťanství tvrdě trestá. Americký server Fox News například loni popsal případ dvojice křesťanských duchovních, kterým hrozil trest smrti. Oficiálně za obvinění ze špionáže, ale podle lidskoprávních organizací byla pravým důvodem zatčení kněží právě jejich křesťanská víra.

Ministerstvo zahraničí případ nekomentuje z obavy, že by mohlo narušit soud v Chartúmu. „Mohu pouze uvést, že v Súdánu řešíme konzulární případ, to je vše," uvedla mluvčí Michaela Lagronová.

◐ Více čtěte na str. 3

While my wife, Vanda, was refueling her car at a gas station, she discovered this headline in DNES, the daily newspaper of the Czech Republic, which says, "Czech held in Sudan faces death penalty." After reading the headline, she left the gas station trembling.
Source: Mladá Fronta Dnes

Outside of Kober prison, the last prison where I was held before my release. When I was taken to Kober, I was terrified the guards would confiscate my Bible, but remarkably, they allowed me to keep it. While there, I taught English to Muslim fellow prisoners using the Gospel of John, praying the message of the Gospel would touch their hearts. Photo by Ebrahim Hamid / AFP / Getty Images

The first picture of me and my family at home after my release from prison. After flying home on a Czech Air Force airplane with the Minister of Foreign Affairs, I was told that I must spend two to three weeks in quarantine in the Central Military Hospital in Prague. But by God's grace, all my medical results were clear, and I was released after just two days in the hospital.

My wife, Vanda, and me on a walk through the historic center of Prague after my release.

Vanda and me at our church in Kladno, Czech Republic, after my release from prison. Our church family had set a reminder on their cellphones to pray for me at 8 p.m. every night—at precisely the time when I would lie down for bed in prison. Their faithful prayers were what allowed me to fall asleep peacefully each night.

During the filming of the Wurmbrand small-group study curriculum in March 2018, I stood in Richard Wurmbrand's solitary cell in Jilava, Romania. Even though it was relatively warm outside, it was still freezing cold in the prison. As I stood there, it became even clearer to me that it was the Lord's protection and provision that helped Richard survive those harsh conditions in prison, which included malnutrition, diseases, beatings, and torture.

On May 11, 2017, my friends Pastor Hassan (right) and Brother Monim (left) were released from prison in Sudan. Hassan was warned that authorities would continue to monitor his activities. Knowing this would put further strain on his family and draw additional scrutiny to the church, he and his family left Sudan. Brother Monim left as well. Both live in a rural town in the eastern United States, where I have had the privilege of meeting with them during my travels to the U.S.

*Since my release from prison, I have traveled around the world,
sharing my testimony of God's provision while I was in prison and
thanking all those who prayed for me and my family. In this photo,
I am sharing at a VOM Advance conference in Tulsa, Oklahoma,
with Pastor Hassan and VOM Radio host Todd Nettleton.*

16

Grudgingly, I removed my clean clothes, not sure when I'd see them again, and changed back into the dingy prison clothes that I'd packed in my suitcase. I pulled out my blanket, a few extra articles of clothing, some shampoo, toilet paper, and my wallet, which I was surprised to discover still contained my Sudanese pounds. The police officials allowed me to remove my medicine—the iron supplements and some antibiotics—and check them into the police reception storage room. I followed the guards into a primitive cell.

The room was fifteen feet wide and eighteen feet long. Fifteen men sat on the floor, which was covered in dirty red carpet. Three of the men were smoking, and the fumes swirled in the musty air. There wasn't enough room for me to walk, so I spread my blanket on the floor and sat cross-legged. But in this position, I knew I could easily get a blood clot, and if that happened, I'd likely die.

Throughout the night, more prisoners arrived until there were more than twenty of us crowded into fewer than three hundred square feet. A fan circulated hot air from beyond the room's only window, and the door to the room was barred. With the hot skin of my cellmates pressed against me, I felt claustrophobic and dirty.

The next morning, I was retrieved from the cell and ushered through the police station and into the office of the "head prosecutor." He smiled, and as I sat on the leather sofa in his air-conditioned office, he arranged for his assistant to bring me a chicken sandwich and a Coke. He also allowed me to use his nail clippers—my nails desperately needed to be trimmed—and when he encouraged me to keep them, I protested and insisted on giving them back. "That's true," he said, "because the next time you need them, you won't be here anymore."

I soon learned that this police station only accepted cases from the NISS prison; it was an extension of the Sudanese Security but not formally under its jurisdiction.

"I'm sure you will only be here for a short while," the prosecutor said. "Soon, everything will be resolved diplomatically, and you will be released."

Maybe this prison won't be too bad after all, I thought, believing the prosecutor's words.

I explained that I had been suffering from anemia, and that I needed to be checked again at the hospital. The next morning, he made the arrangements, and I was transported.

This facility was managed by the Ministry of the Interior, and it seemed to have more equipment than the NISS hospital and may even have been a bit cleaner. I stepped on a scale and was shocked to discover that I had lost fifty-five pounds since December.

The doctor ran more blood work and found that my hemoglobin level was even worse than before. Now, it was half what it should have been. I suspected I might have been bleeding internally. The beatings, coupled with my daily dose of aspirin-based headache relief medicine, made that likely. If I had been home in the Czech Republic, the doctors would have begun cross-matching me for a blood transfusion.

Here in Sudan, though, the doctor made arrangements with the police for me to continue receiving my iron supplements, which I had to pay for on my own, and I returned to the cell.

I I I I I I

Over the next several days, more men were deposited into the stifling cell. There were now roughly two dozen of us sharing the room. I was feeling especially depressed one morning, and I prayed, "How long, Lord, will this last until I am released?" As I passed the time praying, an Eritrean man noticed me and introduced himself. He had a sister who attended an Eritrean church in Khartoum, he told me, but I sensed that he himself was not a born-again follower of Jesus Christ. My suspicions were confirmed when he told me that he had been arrested for trafficking humans through Sudan.

As I shared Christ with him and with other men who temporarily passed through our crowded cell, I began to understand why God had put me in this prison. It was to share the love of Christ with people I never would have met under any other possible circumstances.

One morning, a group of twelve young Eritrean men, two women, and two children were brought into the prison. They had been captured on the Libyan-Sudanese border. The women and children were put into a smaller cell opposite ours; the twelve men were put in our cell, which now held forty-three prisoners, and the conditions continued to deteriorate. In such close proximity to the other men, sleeping was extremely difficult. During the nights, which were unbearably cold, the cell transformed into a large wrestling match with men kicking and hitting each other to steal blankets.

The Eritreans ranged in age from about fourteen to twenty-four years old. During the day, they kept to themselves on one side of the room, smoking and chewing tobacco. The Muslims kept their distance by occupying the other side.

One day, as I was sitting in the corner praying, I sensed God speaking to me. His voice was not audible, but I felt the Holy Spirit guiding my heart and saying, "Go and sit beside these people and tell them about Jesus."

I chose to obey and walked across the room. As soon as I sat down, two Eritrean men who spoke English immediately asked me questions about where I was from and what I was doing in prison. Without fear of the Muslims, I began talking openly about Jesus Christ. I shared my testimony with them, describing my journey to faith, and then I encouraged them to accept Jesus Christ as their personal Savior. These men, I learned, belonged to an Orthodox church, but without icons on the wall to kiss and pray to, there was no evidence of their religion.

As the conversations deepened, God sent a pervasive peace into my heart. "Now I see what You want me to do here," I prayed. God brought results I could not even have imagined! The Eritrean men who spoke English began interpreting for the rest of the group, and over the course of the afternoon and evening, as more and more prisoners joined our conversation, *all twelve of the men* accepted Christ as their Savior.

The next morning, the group of young Eritreans was ushered out of the cell and transferred to another prison. I never saw them again. My heart was full, though, knowing that God had done such a tremendous work in their lives and that He had allowed me to be part of it. *This* was the purpose of my imprisonment, I finally realized. *This* was the answer to my prayer. In that moment, my mindset changed. No longer did I worry about my well-being or safety. God had put me there for a reason: to be His light, to spread the Gospel message. From that moment on, I resolved to worry no longer about what would happen to me. The future was in God's hands, and that day, and every day, my mission was to be Christ's light, no matter how dark the cell.

I began sharing the Gospel with everyone God put in my way. I had to stay sharp around the Muslims. Some of them were confidants of the NISS, secret police informers who would report back to the Sudanese Security with information that would help them in their investigation of me.

"Oh, you are an American," they said after listening to me speak English. I knew they would try to glean information about me and trap me, so I usually replied, "I am not American; I am Czech." There were spies everywhere, but I learned to identify them by their many suspicious questions, and usually my suspicions were confirmed when they were removed from our crowded cell after only a few days.

When the number of men reached forty, I grew thankful that the ceiling in the cell was relatively high. If it had been lower, I'm not sure any of us could have survived. The lack of space had become an acute problem, especially during the day when the temperature was sweltering. I knew it must have been well over one hundred degrees. There was a fan outside the room that kept the air from becoming completely stagnant, but it functioned intermittently and never kept us cool. When I was able, I wove through the sweaty bodies to catch some fresh air at the window. I also discovered that if I made my way to the barred door, I could feel a bit of a breeze. I no longer had the option of lying down on the floor and instead, constantly chose between sitting with my legs crossed or standing. Standing was less painful, so I spent much of the day standing on my feet, shoulder to shoulder with the other prisoners who were just as miserable as I was.

The hunger was unrelenting, and I felt it gnawing at my stomach constantly. Twice each day, we received boiled beans to eat. Unlike the *fuhl* in the NISS prison, these beans were flavorless. They arrived in one large bowl, along with a plastic bag of round, moldy Sudanese bread. We needed the bread in order to scoop the beans, but there was never enough for all of us to share. Since the Sudanese use their left hands to wash their bottoms, they use only their right hands to eat with. I was careful to use only my right hand to eat from the communal bowl as well, lest I cause offense or my fellow prisoners would think I was contaminating the food.

Sometimes, the first meal arrived at 11:00 a.m., but at other times, it came hours later. The second serving of beans and bread arrived sometime after dark. I needed to have some food with which to take my iron supplements, so if I could, I tried to save a piece of bread for the morning, just in case the first meal was late. I remembered how terrible the food was that I shared with my ISIS cellmates in the NISS prison, but now I found myself desperately longing for it.

A soiled and putrid red carpet stretched across our cell. There were two toilets outside, and twice a day, the guards unlocked the door and allowed us to use them. There were two guards who took pity on me because of my ill-treatment and sometimes allowed me to go first, but the other guards deliberately made me wait until all of the other prisoners had finished relieving themselves. It seemed to be a regular occurrence for the police station to be without running water, and I was often forced to add my portion to the huge pile of excrement already stockpiled in the overflowing toilet. There was a small bar of soap, but if I washed my hands too quickly, it slipped from my hands and fell to the filthy floor.

During the first three days I was there, the prosecutors told me, "If you don't like these conditions, you have to submit a written complaint, and we will try to send you back to the security prison."

The thought of returning to the NISS prison was very appealing to me, and I asked my new cellmates if I should submit the formal complaint. "Whatever you do, don't go back," they warned me. "You will get used to this."

I had only been at the police station for one week when a representative from the Swiss Embassy came to check on me. He had a lengthy discussion with the prosecutors and told me that Mr. Sláma wouldn't be able to visit me on April 8, as scheduled, but that the Swiss were overseeing my case.

| | | | | | |

When I arrived at the Niyaba Mendola police station, I knew the investigation by the Sudanese prosecutors would likely continue, but I still waited for nearly a month. "Maybe tomorrow we will come," the officers said, again and again. Each day, I grew more and more restless. Anxiety overwhelmed me as I battled the stench of the overcrowded cell, and I wondered if I would ever be released.

The investigation into my "crimes" finally resumed on April 20. I entered the investigation room and sat across the table from a prosecutor, expecting more of the same questions I'd been dodging since December.

I glanced down at the table to a thick folder that was open in front of him, and I saw an alphabetical list of names. My eyes flew down the list, and in seconds, I knew that these were the men who participated in the Christian conference in Addis Ababa. Instantly, I knew that in addition to the government moles sent to spy on the conference, one of the conference attendees must have been an informant as well. *How else would the Sudanese government have this list of names?*

The prosecutor began asking me about the participants. "Do you know John Martin?" he asked.

My answers were simple because I knew that any information I gave him would incriminate both me and the Christians on the list. "I might know a John," I said. "I don't remember. Maybe he was from America?" I did my best to appear cooperative without revealing any real information. Besides, the prosecutor already knew the answer.

"Was there a Korean Christian?"

"As far as I can remember," I said, "there might have been one Asian person. I don't know." The questions continued, one after another.

Finally, knowing this interrogation was bearing no fruit, the prosecutor closed the folder and stood. I was ushered back to the cell as he walked away.

17

From my first visit with the Czech consular officer, I understood it would likely take three months for my case to be resolved. But by mid-April, I had been imprisoned in Sudan for four and a half months.

When I was finally summoned to the court, I heard my charges for the first time. There were several leveled against me, but only two of them stood out in my mind—the two that carried with them a sentence of death. I knew in my mind that it was unlikely a foreigner would be put to death, but hearing the words certainly caused me to raise my eyebrows. I thought about my family, about how they would receive the news of my threatened execution. I could imagine my wife's tears, my children's sadness, my congregation's sorrow.

I was also impacted by the threat of serving a life sentence, which was a very real possibility in my situation. My lawyer looked at me and saw the distress and fear in my eyes. I tried to imagine what it would be like living the rest of my life in a Sudanese prison, never seeing my wife, daughter, son, or other family members again. Even spending twenty more years in prison would feel impossible to handle. The best outcome, the one I most hoped for, was for the Sudanese government to sentence me to time served and no more. This seemed to be a frequent occurrence among similar cases in the country, and if it were to happen, I would be a free man.

In those moments, I thought about the Apostle Peter, and not only because I shared his name. After the Lord's resurrection, when He was meeting with the disciples, Jesus asked Peter three times, "Do you love me?" What Jesus said after Peter's response was what I thought of at that time: "When you were young, you used to dress yourself and walk wherever you wanted, but when you are old, you will stretch out your hands, and another will dress you and carry you where you do not want to go" (John 21:18). Prison was the place I did not want to go, but of this I was confident: the Lord put me there, and He had his reasons, no matter the outcome.

I I I I I I

When I returned from the court, I saw that the guards had moved me from the crowded cell into a smaller, solitary one that was six and a half feet wide and thirteen feet long. Unlike my first experience in solitary confinement in the Refrigerator at the NISS prison, this time, my cell was scorching hot. The ceiling was much lower than the larger room I'd come from—so low, in fact, that I could touch it—and large, gray wall tiles insulated the room, trapping the sweltering heat from the day inside the small space.

Also, unlike my first experience in solitary confinement, my cell here was not truly solitary. There was a larger room across the corridor from mine filled with more prisoners, and if I raised my voice, I thought I might be able to talk to the men across the hall. Some of them reminded me of Hassan and Rev. Kuwa Shamal, who had also attended the conference in Addis Ababa, and I prayed for my Sudanese brothers once more.

It was so hot in the small cell that my sweat immediately evaporated from my skin and I was left with salt crystals on my forehead and body. Dust blew in from outside, and many mornings, I had to clean myself with a small broom lying in the corner.

At night, I tried to sleep on my blanket, but each morning, I woke up with my face pressed against the red carpet, stained with all manner of dirt, urine, and excrement, which covered the floor. Somehow, even in those difficult circumstances, I was able to fall quickly into a deep, peaceful sleep. Inexplicably, for my entire time in the NISS prison as well as at the Niyaba Mendola police station, I was able to sleep peacefully.

Sometimes, I knew that my dreams were the result of my tired brain and exhausted imagination. But at other times, I felt that God was directly communicating with me. In one dream, I saw my passport returned to me. It was worn out and almost falling apart. *What does this mean? God, are you telling me that my imprisonment will be longer than I am expecting?*

| | | | | |

At the end of April, Mr. Sláma visited me once more in the police station. He told me that within a few months, he would be reassigned by the Czech government and would no longer be stationed in Cairo. I felt thankful for his kindness and for comforting my family through his communication with them, and I prayed that my next advocate would be as edifying as Mr. Sláma had been to me.

On this visit, Mr. Sláma brought the best surprise yet—a third letter from my family and a Czech Bible! I couldn't believe my eyes. He explained that my Bible was a gift from the incoming consular officer, prompted by my family back home in the Czech Republic. I would finally be able to hold God's precious Word in my hands and digest its beautiful promises. I was the happiest I'd been since my arrest in December, and this single gesture brought my friendship with Mr. Sláma to an even deeper level.

For the first time, I was also allowed to keep the letter from my family. After my final visit with Mr. Sláma, I tucked it inside into my Bible, returned to my cell, and sat down on the floor to read. But without my reading glasses, I wasn't able to make much progress, even if I squinted. The words in the Bible were just too small.

Two days later, I finally managed to retrieve my glasses from my stored luggage, along with a pen, and I sneaked them back to my cell. With my eyesight restored, I used the marginal space on my letter to record thoughts about my Bible reading. Soon, the letter was covered with scripture references, prayers, and insights the Lord was giving me. I had absolutely no idea how long I would be able to keep the Bible, so I began memorizing verses with a ravenous appetite.

From 8:00 a.m. until 4:30 or even 5:00 p.m. each afternoon, enough sunlight poured into my cell for me to read. I propped my Bible against the bars on either the door or the window and read it for as long as I could. Never had I been so hungry to feast on God's Word. It only took me three weeks to read from Genesis all the way to Revelation. I memorized any verse that stuck out and spoke to me. The Psalms were particularly comforting, and so were verses like 1 Corinthians 10:13: "No test has overtaken you that is not common to man. God is faithful, and he will not let you be tried beyond your ability, but with the test he will also provide the way of escape, that you may be able to endure it."

Soon, I established a Bible reading plan. On Monday, I read the Gospel of Matthew, and on Tuesday, I read Mark. On Wednesday, I made my way through Luke before turning, on Thursday, to John. When Friday arrived, I was ready for the book of Acts, and then the next day, I moved on to Romans. Each day, I pored over a new book of the Bible, and this intensive approach to reading the Bible gave me a profoundly new understanding of the whole of Scripture.

I began to understand the Bible from completely different perspectives. Passages that I thought I had understood now became new and fresh to me, and passages that I hadn't understood became clear. Wherever I opened the Bible, whether in the Old Testament or the New Testament, the Holy Spirit revealed deep truth from the verses. Secretly, I used the pen from my luggage and the letter from my family to make notes about this wonderful, revealing truth. Each day, I was continually amazed that I was able to spend so much time with God's Word, and I wondered why I had this privilege of not doing anything but reading my Bible.

Just before Ramadan, several young English-speaking students from the police academy were brought into the prison to be trained alongside the older guards. When the older guards were sitting at the reception and no one was watching, some of the cadets were very friendly to me, and I had several opportunities to share the Gospel with them.

"What are you reading?" a young guard asked.

"I am reading the Bible," I said.

"What is the Bible?"

"The Bible is 'Injil,'" the Arabic name for the Gospel of Jesus, I told him.

Another guard joined the conversation. "What is the difference between the Bible and the Koran?" he asked. This was just the question I needed to be able to tell them about how Christ died, how He loves them, and how Jesus is the only way to God. The two guards were receptive to the Gospel, and at the end of the conversation, they told me they were eager to hear more. I was delighted that the Lord continued to use me in such a powerful way, even in prison.

I   I   I   I   I   I

Six weeks later, Mr. Sláma arrived for our last meeting. He brought me another letter from home, a personal letter from my wife that had been transcribed into English by our daughter. I unfolded the letter, put on my glasses, and began reading.

Dear Petr,

Last week we got new information about you, that you were able to read our letters. So we will send you letters more often.

I have hidden your letter, I read it often, and I am really glad that it is handwritten by you.

I noticed that Vanda had included several significant, hidden details in the letter. After updating me on the advent of spring in the Czech Republic, on the wellbeing of the family dog, and on Vanda's parents, she wrote, *"We have regular visits from the English teacher and her husband."* I knew this referred to VOM's deputy regional director for Africa whom I had been training. He had assumed responsibility over much of my work in Africa while I had been imprisoned.

Vanda also mentioned that *"Uncle who is teaching Vanda hematology will come for a visit again,"* referring to my VOM assistant, Keith, a dear friend whom I'd known since my days working in the medical field and who was now caring for my family and aiding with my responsibilities while I was away. I was relieved to read, *"His friends up north say that they have had a lot of snow making everything white"* because I knew this was code that Vanda was using to explain that VOM, Keith's "friends up north" in North America, had cleaned all of the accounts and passwords that connected me to them.

Vanda concluded the letter with words that stirred my emotions. She said she was praying for me all the time, missed me, wished peace for me, and hoped I would be coming home soon. She remembered all the beautiful moments we had spent together over the years. At night, just before she fell asleep, she said she kept me in her mind, and each morning, she awoke to send greetings to me "through the first sunbeam."

The letter wasn't long, and she explained that instead of using pen and ink, she hoped to speak with me face-to-face soon. But what

Vanda wrote next reminded me of why I fell in love with her in the first place, why she caught my eye at the hospital, why I married her, why I love her with all my heart. "Even in this hard situation," she said, "we are not alone. We are in God's hand." She ended the letter with, "Sending a big hug and many kisses, Your Vanda."

In the presence of Mr. Sláma and the prosecutor in the Niyaba Mendola police station, I was allowed to compose a second letter to my family, again in English.

My dear ones,

Thanks a lot for your letters; I was very encouraged by them. I am glad that you are doing well. I am doing well too. The Lord is with me here all the time, and He is using me for His kingdom. I am having a great time with the Lord and am praying for all of you all the time.

This test is not beyond our strength, and the Lord is faithful and righteous and has prepared an outcome for us. Please be strong in the Lord and trust Him that He is in control, He is the one who has the keys to my cell.

Thanks also for the medicines that you sent to me in February. I still have plenty of them. My health is stable and I am slowly building up hemoglobin. Otherwise, I am at full strength and am walking a lot in my cell every day.

I appreciate your prayers very much. I cannot tell enough how I love you all and how I miss you.

I hope that for all the prayers, I will be able to be released soon.

Please greet all the family, friends, brothers and sisters and coworkers.

With a great love,
In Him,
Petr

| | | | | | |

On May 5, Pastor Hassan and Monim were transferred from the NISS prison to the cell directly across from mine. I was delighted, and they were just as surprised to see me because, as I learned, they assumed I had been released when they saw the guard at the NISS prison lead me by their cell down to the storage room to collect my suitcase on March 29. Ten days later, Pastor Kuwa arrived also.

It had been over a month since I had seen these brothers, and I was eager for their fellowship. At times, the police officers allowed them to stand outside my solitary cell, and we talked to each other in hushed voices. I learned in May that Pastor Hassan had been able to receive a New Testament from some members of his family. I was thankful that he, too, now had God's Word to lean on and learn from in prison.

Many times, even though we were locked in separate cells, we shared verses of encouragement with each other. Our cells were only about fifteen feet apart, but the roar of the fan was deafening. "Read Romans 8:18!" I yelled, not caring who heard me. "For I consider that the sufferings of this present time are not worth comparing with the glory that is to be revealed to us." It was a verse I had used to encourage my family, and now I used it to encourage my friends.

Brother Monim would participate in our quiet conversations about Scripture, but he did not yell out Bible verses or read the Bible in front of other prisoners. While Kuwa and Hassan's families were Christians from the Nuba Mountains, Monim had been born into a Muslim family, and therefore in the eyes of other Muslims and Sudan's Islamist government, he was a Muslim. That meant that, if it was discovered that he was a Christian, the capital charge of *apostasy* could be added to whatever other charges he faced, in addition to the threats from Muslims who were fellow prisoners. Because of this, he kept his faith private while he was in prison. In fact, at the next-to-last prison where we were held, some Muslims asked Monim to serve as the imam!

Later, Kuwa and Hassan explained to me that they always advise new believers from Muslim families to be cautious and thoughtful about how and when they share the news of their faith in Christ with their families. Being in prison and on trial only added to this challenge for Monim.

Two weeks later, a guard delivered a gift from the Swiss consular officer. Inside the package were two bottles of shampoo and a Czech translation of Paul Johnson's book *Jesus: A Biography from a Believer*. As I opened the cover, I saw a letter from my family that had been tucked inside the jacket of the book. "We are really glad that you are in better condition and you are able to get better food," I read.

Of course, this was not true. It was what had been relayed to them via the head prosecutor and the consular officer after his April visit with me, but the reality was that I was in a much worse condition. My meals had been reduced from four times a day to only two, and rats ran through my cell at night.

In nearly every aspect, the conditions inside this police station were much worse than any I had experienced so far, but with regular access to my attorney and with the possibility of using my Sudanese currency to purchase necessities, the Swiss consular officer had told my family that my condition had improved. I took comfort in knowing that my family would not worry as much about me now.

I continued reading the letter and learned that my church family had been fasting and held regular prayer time every evening at 8:00 p.m. I stopped reading and quickly calculated the time difference between Prague and Khartoum. *Eight o'clock ... that's exactly when I lie down for bed!* I knew that my church's faithful prayers were what had allowed me to fall asleep peacefully each night.

There was a second letter tucked inside the book jacket, and as I pulled it out, I was delighted to see that Váva had enclosed her own personal letter to me as well. While reading her words, I found myself admiring how much responsibility my little girl had been able to shoulder while I had been imprisoned in Sudan.

She told me that our son Petr was writing his bachelor's thesis and had allowed enough time not to be stressed at the last minute. Váva also said that what I wrote in my letter had been really encouraging to her. The whole family was encouraged, she explained. "Your letter gives Mom new energy." I was thrilled to hear this. Even when I was so far away, imprisoned in Sudan, I could still support my family and bring them joy.

Vanda's birthday was coming up soon—the first of her birthdays I would not be able to attend in all the many years of our marriage. The very thought saddened me, but I was pleased to learn that Petr and Váva had picked out the perfect birthday present for her. They had decided to buy their mother a brand-new phone because she spent so much time calling people these days. I couldn't help but smile. I imagined my daughter teaching Vanda how to operate the new gadget, the new "innovation," as Váva described it in her letter.

My wife missed me very much, and I thought of her trying to conceal her emotions around the children. "Sometimes she tries to hide them in front of me and my brother," Váva explained, "but she is not successful." I could picture Vanda in my mind. I saw her face drop when she became suddenly overwhelmed with feelings of loneliness and helplessness. I could see her trying to be strong for our children while struggling to suppress the pain of my absence. It brought me some relief that my children were there for her, keeping her company, comforting her, sharing her burden. If Vanda were alone and forced to handle this situation all by herself, I didn't think she could cope. My daughter saw her reading the Bible and also the letters of Jan (John) Hus—a Czech theologian and church reformer who lived in Prague in the beginning of the fifteenth century, nearly a hundred years before the Protestant Reformation started in Germany. Jailed in Constance for writing and preaching against the un-Scriptural excesses of Rome, he penned his "Letters from

Constance" as he waited to be burned at the stake in 1415. And now, Hus's words written from a prison cell six hundred years ago were encouraging my Vanda as she waited and worried about her husband—locked in a prison cell in 2016.

Other family members and friends from our church were also supporting my wife, I learned. I knew they must have been talking with her daily and praying for us without ceasing.

I smiled as I thought of my son, and I wished I could have been home to encourage him as he wrote. As Váva updated me on her own progress, I remembered my own first job in a hospital, so many years ago. She'd landed a job at the hospital in Prague, she said, but the commute to work took about an hour. Traveling by bus would be one option, but her fiancé, Honza, had offered to let her borrow his car. "He is also really helpful here; he started to water our trees in the garden, so there starts to be small apricots. We also pray together for you and for your release."

Váva also told me she had been in daily contact with VOM staff, who were helping with the expenses. She must have assumed I'd be thinking about that, wondering how my family would be able to pay the mortgage, handle the finances, and so on. To read my daughter's words—that "everything is covered"—was tremendously reassuring. To know she was in frequent contact with her "uncle" Keith, who was "giving us big support," was also an answer to my prayers.

Váva sent an update on the health of one of my friends—a friend for whom the Lord had already prompted me to pray—and then concluded her letter with an assurance that my family remained in close contact with the Ministry of Foreign Affairs and with the embassy in Cairo and that they were in the final stages of securing another attorney for me.

Don't worry about it, she wrote. *Miss you, father.*
Your daughter Vanda, as well as wife Vanda and Petr

I finished reading the letter and immediately called to the guard to ask him for some paper. Surprisingly, he agreed to find me some, and I soon began writing a secret letter to my family from my cell. I didn't know when, or even if, I would be able to send it.

I got very encouraged by your letters, especially by the prayer support every day in our church and the fasting chain! I am sure that Keith's friends up north do the same.

I can tell you how much I rejoiced when I received the Czech Bible during the last Embassy visit! In the first two weeks, I have read through more than half of it! After five months, I was so hungry for the Word of God! I am getting encouraged, especially by the Psalms.

Our Lord is teaching me to be patient in this situation (see Romans 12:12). As I wrote in my previous letter, He is giving us strength to pass this test successfully (see 1 Corinthians 10:13). I am having a great time with the Lord every day. Since April 20, I have been alone in my cell again, so I can read, pray, and sing aloud. The Lord is reminding me of the words of many songs that I learned when I was young and under the Communist oppression in our country.

When I read the Bible now and I find a verse that the Lord had put on my mind during the first five months here, it is as if I have found a lost pearl! I was also encouraged very much by reading the passage of 1 Peter 4:12–14. I am sure you will be encouraged by it as well!

I am also very thankful to the Lord when I hear about the excellent studies of our daughter, Vanda, and son, Petr. I am really proud of you, children! I am also glad that your mom has started to learn English seriously with a very good teacher. You will need it, Vanda, as you will have to travel with me in the future after I am released so that you would not need to worry about me! :-)

Physically, I am doing well. I feel well and strong though I have lost twenty kilos. My blood pressure seems to be normal.

Things are moving very slowly here, so we need to be patient and trust the Lord as He is the one who is holding the keys.

I have put all my hope in Him, not in men. He is the one in control. We all are in His loving hands and the King's care!

I cannot express in words how I cherish you all in my heart! I miss you very much! I rejoice in the hope of seeing you soon and being with you at home! I am keeping you all in my fervent prayers every day whenever I pause the reading of the Bible. I pray for you and bless you all (Numbers 6:24–26).

With much love,
Petr

Then I took a small piece of paper and recorded a list of needed items—things like a pumice file for scraping the dead skin from my feet, various toiletries, and anti-mold and anti-bacterial cream. I folded the piece of paper into a small square and waited for the Swiss consular officer's visit.

Five days later, on May 24, he arrived. As I was led from my cell to talk with him, I held the small square of paper carefully in my hand. When I held out my hand to shake his, I slipped the carefully folded list into it. When he left the meeting, I prayed for my letter, and my list, as they began their journey to Europe.

18

In May and June, the temperature during the day rose above 120 degrees, even inside the building. I was occupying a small solitary confinement cell that previously had been designated to hold women. I was thankful to be alone in my cell because I could wear the shorts I retrieved from my luggage. If I were still in the larger cell, my Muslim cellmates would have considered me immodest because my knees would be visible. The heat was oppressive, though, and even in shorts, I felt miserable.

On May 21, I heard that twelve members of an outlawed human rights group had arrived at the police station. One of them, a woman who was nursing a baby, was released the same day. Nine men were squeezed into the main cell. Since I was occupying the solitary cell normally designed for women, the other two women were kept in one of the offices before being moved into the reception area of the police station, sleeping in the same room with the guards who normally sat and watched television. The racially diverse group hearkened from different tribes. Some of them came from al-Bashir's governing group, the Shaigiya tribe, although they did not always agree with he Sudanese president. There was a Cameroonian woman who had worked as an office intern. Almost all of them were Sudanese, highly intelligent, educated, with vast international experiences.

The leader of this group—because he had a heart condition and was suffocating in the overcrowded room—bribed a policeman to be brought into my solitary cell. He spoke fluent English, and I enjoyed having a conversational partner. When his attorneys brought him extra food—yogurt, sandwiches, tea bags—he shared it with me, and for three weeks, I lived in luxury.

One other member of this group was a reporter who worked for the International Criminal Court, which was a very dangerous job. Anyone connected with the ICC was viewed as a traitor in Sudan because President Bashir had been criminally charged by it with committing war crimes and crimes against humanity. The reporter told me that he had been arrested during his visit to Khalafala Afifi after his office was raided by the Sudanese government security forces. The NISS officers had planted homosexual pornography on the laptop of a third male member of their group. The government brought charges against all of them for criticizing President al-Bashir, for monitoring the elections in Sudan, and for educating and training the Sudanese people in ways to fight for the right to vote.

As I read my Bible, my cellmate read his Koran. Like the other prisoners in Niyaba Mendola, though, he seemed to be a moderate Muslim, not a militant Muslim like my ISIS cellmates in the NISS prison. When he came across interesting passages in his Koran, he asked me questions about what the Bible said on the topic. Every day, I prayed for the Lord to open this man's heart and reveal Himself as Savior, Lord, and God.

When one of the NISS officers realized that we were enjoying spending the days talking in English, he became enraged and ordered my cellmate to be moved out. I felt the loss tremendously, and for the rest of the summer, I was alone in my room.

| | | | | |

On June 12, in the Niyaba Mendola police station, I received another visit from the Swiss consular officer. He brought me another word from my family. I learned that when they received my letter from May 19, they had been "enormously encouraged" and "cried as we read your words!" My family even found and read all the Bible verses I referenced—"really strong words that fit your situation." One of the verses was Luke 18:7: "And will not God give justice to his elect, who cry to him day and night? Will he delay long over them?" They were overjoyed to learn that I finally had a Bible to read; they called it "a miracle that was sent to you from heaven," and they thanked God for all the people who participated on the Bible's journey to me. Every day, I thanked God for delivering to me the life-giving words of Scripture—words that had comforted so many men and women over the centuries who found themselves, like me, suffering for the sake of Christ.

In the letter, I learned that my family was praying for me, not only at church but also specifically at eight o'clock during prayer time at home. The pastor of our church preached a sermon on Sunday, May 29, that was especially meaningful for my family. They "were able to feel God's closeness" that morning and were really encouraged to remember the words of Luke 18:1 when Jesus told His disciples a parable to show them that they should always pray and not lose heart or give up. As I read these words, I also felt the closeness of God. I was reminded of the power of prayer and the fact that no matter where God's children find themselves—in a cell or in a sanctuary— each of us can boldly approach the throne of grace to discover a Father who loves us and gives us His undivided attention.

"We miss you a lot," the letter read, "and we can't wait to see you. We really wish that you could be with us. Everybody is sending greetings to you, thinking about you, and they don't weaken in their prayers." Vanda explained that she was very afraid and anxious for me, but after reading my letter, God's peace filled her, and her heart became calm. I was thankful to know that my family had been able to secure all the items I included on the list of things I needed and that they would be sending them to me as soon as possible. I put the letter down and rubbed the top of my head, reflecting on my wife's last sentence: "We really want to be all together at home." She also referenced a timely Bible verse about Jesus's own attitude about suffering in the Garden of Gethsemane, Mark 14:36: " 'Abba, Father,' he said, 'all things are possible for you. Remove this cup from me. Yet not what I will, but what you will.' "

My dear friend and assistant, Keith, added a final note of his own to the end of the letter. It brought me great encouragement to read his words: "If one member suffers, all suffer together; if one member is honored, all rejoice together" (1 Corinthians 12:26). Through Keith, the Lord had encouraged me greatly, reminding me that others were sharing in my suffering. I was not amputated from the universal body of believers, the body of Jesus Christ in this world. No, I was part of that body, an extension of it here in Sudan. And joy filled my heart to know that other Christians were praying for me even as I sat and suffered in that prison.

Again, I responded joyfully to their letter.

My beloved ones,

I was really deeply encouraged by your letter that I have received today! Thanks for all the words and verses of encouragement. I finished my reading of the whole Bible in three weeks and started the second time through, so I gain a lot of joy (Psalm 62:6), strength (Psalm 86:16), hope (Psalm 62:6) and comfort (Psalm 94:19) from the Scriptures, especially from the Psalms! My heart is full of gratitude to the Lord for all His goodness to me as well as to our family. I read especially Psalm 103:1–6 with tears of gratefulness quite often and memorized almost the whole

*of Psalm 103. I am sure you are getting encouraged through it
as well.*

*In fact, the current situation cannot be compared with the
future glory which should be revealed in us (Romans 8:18). I
continue to pray for all of you, especially in spirit as He intercedes
for us with unspeakable words according to God's will (Romans
8:26–28). Also, we know that to those who love God, everything
works for good!*

I paused and considered how I could tell them about the opportunities I was having to share the Gospel with the men in the cell near
me. Using coded language that the police officers would not understand, I thought of the verse in the parable of the sower—"some of the
seeds fell into the fertile soil."

*In the past three weeks, I have been experiencing the Ephe-
sians 6:15 again. I pray Matthew 13:23 will happen soon.*

| | | | | |

My visits with the Swiss consular officer and Mr. Sláma in the
police station continued throughout the summer, and through them,
I was able to continue sending and receiving letters to and from
my wife, daughter, and son. The Swiss consular officer also delivered
a package from my family full of all of the necessities I'd requested.
I was continually amazed by the many ways God was taking care of me.

Over the next month and a half, Váva graduated from medical
school and became a physician, and my son, Petr, earned his bachelor's degree. I was saddened to miss these occasions, but because
I knew that the Lord had a purpose for my imprisonment, I was also
confident in His plan for my family's life. God had shown Himself
to be faithful time and time again, and I knew he would not aban-
don us now. Váva's medical school graduation was a day I had

dreamed of three years before my arrest in the harrowing premonition that foretold it. Now the dream had come true, first in seeing the door at the NISS prison and now when I really did miss her graduation because of my imprisonment. And now I had missed my son's as well.

On one of the visits from Mr. Sláma, he delivered another package from my family, and in this one, there was a hymnal. I was overjoyed at the sight of the precious book. *A Bible and now a hymnal—what blessings!* As usual, I signed for the items in the presence of the consular officer, but I was devastated when the prosecutor didn't allow me to take the items back to my cell. I returned empty-handed and deeply frustrated.

Later in the day, another one of the police academy students arrived and told me the chief prosecutor wished to see me in his office. When I walked into the room, I saw him examining each item from the package from my family. "What's this?" he asked, holding up the hymnal.

"It's a collection of songs."

"Can you sing?"

"Of course I can," I responded.

"Then sing me a song," he ordered. I was determined to make the most of this opportunity to share the Gospel with the prosecutor and the police academy student, so I decided to sing the wonderful hymn that the Holy Spirit had given to me during my first night in solitary confinement: Handel's "Thine Be the Glory." For three verses, I sang as the prosecutor and student listened.

I finished the song but was hesitant to give up so quickly, so I began talking. "Let me now tell you what this song is all about!" I said, and I shared the Gospel with the two men, grateful to have yet another opportunity to tell the Muslim guards the truth of Jesus Christ. Back in my cell, I smiled. This experience had made me feel like the Israelites after they were taken into Babylonian captivity: "For there our captors required of us songs, and our tormentors, mirth, saying, 'Sing us one of the songs of Zion!'" (Psalm 137:3). I knew that as long as the Lord allowed, I would keep singing.

On July 18, following a visit from the Swiss consular officer and his new colleague, I wrote another letter to my family, encouraging them to stand firm in our adversity, to remember that we were not suffering in vain because God had a great purpose He was working through our pain. I told them I was doing well and constantly rejoicing in the presence of the Lord as I used my time in prison to study the Word of God. Since May 1, I had read the Old Testament three times and was on my fifth reading of the New Testament. And the Lord was still showing me something new!

I found a great source of peace, joy, strength, and hope in thanking God, even for this difficulty, because in all circumstances, the Bible tells us, we should give Him thanks (1 Thessalonians 5:18). I reminded my family that as we waited on the Lord, we should stand firm in our faith and have a brave heart (Psalm 31:24) because we trust that we are firmly held and protected in His loving hands (Psalm 139:5). God is the only one in control, not us. And the Lord has His own ways of working His mysterious, sovereign will. And even when we couldn't see or understand them, our hearts should reach out to praise Him even now, to praise Him for His intervention (Psalm 109:30–31).

It was a wonderful thing to know that while I sat in the cell and waited, God was active and on the move. He could turn the hearts of the people in power in Sudan wherever He wanted (Proverbs 21:1). While we suffered this hardship, God was faithfully helping us, preserving us, comforting us so that we could one day comfort others who faced similar situations (2 Corinthians 1:3–7). In my letter, I urged my family to remember that this short and light tribulation, though painful at the moment for all of us, would produce an immense weight of eternal glory (2 Corinthians 4:17–18).

"You are always on my heart and mind," I wrote at the end of the letter. "I am praying and praising God for you all the time and can't wait to see you all at home soon and to be with you!"

| | | | | | |

Despite enjoying my time of personal Bible study in solitary confinement and the ability to sing the wonderful, deep hymns of faith, sometimes moments of sadness and self-pity invaded my heart and mind. Even though I had already learned how to overcome these feelings by proclaiming that the Lord was my peace and joy, the emotions still overwhelmed me at times.

One afternoon, as I was indulging in self-pity, my mind was suddenly interrupted by a vision on the wall of my cell. In a quick flash, I saw the faces of three Eritrean friends named Haile Naizgi, Dr. Kiflu, and Kidane Woldu. They were Christian church leaders whom I had met several years earlier on a trip to Eritrea, and they were all still in prison for their Christian witness and church activities. Most likely, they had spent countless numbers of those days trapped in shipping containers where it was unbearably hot during the day and frigid cold at night. For *twelve years*, they had suffered in prison.

As quickly as it came, the image on the wall disappeared, but the Lord's message to me remained clear: "Why are you complaining? Why are you feeling sorry for yourself? You've been in prison for just over six months—what about them? What about your brothers from Eritrea?" From that day forward, I included these three dear fellow prisoners in my fervent prayers, asking the Lord to be with them in their suffering. Throughout my imprisonment, the Lord put on my mind other Christian prisoners, men and women from China, North Korea, and Central Asia. As I prayed for the great cloud of witnesses of these bold believers, my own daily cross became lighter and lighter.

| | | | | | |

Mr. Sláma soon visited again, and that time, he had come to tell me goodbye. It was his last trip to Sudan before he left for his new post in Australia. We met in the head prosecutor's office as usual—but after several minutes, the prosecutor suddenly left the room.

Mr. Sláma abruptly stood. He pulled his cell phone from his pocket and slipped it into my hand. "Here is my phone," he said. "Talk to your family."

I frantically punched in the numbers. For thirty seconds, I was able to hear my daughter's voice. Mere seconds after I hung up, the chief prosecutor returned to the office, and the unusual situation became clear to me: He had intended to allow me to make this phone call all along. It was a beautiful moment of grace in the midst of a terrible situation.

❙ ❙ ❙ ❙ ❙ ❙

I marked the anniversary of my arrest on the tenth of each month, wondering when my case would be sent to the courts. *Lord, how long will I have to be here?* As I slept, the Lord provided an answer to my question. At the end of scorching July, I had another dream in which I was walking beside a man on a long road that led up a steep hill. This man was the newly appointed consular officer who was supposed to replace Mr. Sláma at the beginning of September. I began asking him about his Arabic. *God, are You letting me know that You will send me an Arabic-speaking consular officer who better understands the court sessions?* As the dream continued, snow began to fall on our heads as we walked along. *Why snow? God, are You telling me that instead of being released in July, August, or September, I will be freed in January or February?*

All summer, I remained in prison. Only one of the toilets functioned, and the shower stopped working, too, so in order to wash ourselves, we rinsed with water from the tap. After it rained, however, the water came out brown and dirty. We poured it into a bucket, waited until the mud settled to the bottom, and then carefully decanted the water into another container. The process was painstaking but essential, and so far, the water had not made any of us ill.

One day, though, I decided to clean the bucket, which had become filthy from being stored near the toilet. Not long after, my right hand became infected—the hand I used to scrub the bucket. The infection soon spread all over my body. It covered my skin and irritated the hair follicles on my arms and legs. My whole body was itching terribly. I remembered Job when his body was covered with loathsome sores from the sole of his foot to the crown of his head and he scraped himself while he sat in the ashes (Job 2:7–8).

On August 3, the Ministry of Justice conducted an inspection of the Niyaba Mendola police station. Through their lawyer, the human rights group had complained about the inhumane conditions, and now the highest-ranking prosecutor had arrived to see things for himself.

As he walked throughout the building, surveying the conditions of the prisoners, he stopped and looked through the bars of my cell door.

"Is everything all right?" he asked. At last! An opportunity had arisen for me to plead my case.

"Honestly," I said, "nothing is all right here. I've been kept here for four months already, and we are still waiting for the court." The man listened in silence and then walked away.

The next morning, a guard arrived at my cell. "Take all your things," he said. "You are being transferred to another prison." I was astonished that the prosecutor had acted on my behalf, and I quickly gathered my clothes, toiletries, Bible, hymnal, and glasses, and walked out of the solitary cell.

Within minutes, Pastor Hassan and the others joined me, and together we left the police station. At that point, it didn't matter where we would be taken. Anywhere must surely be better than the Niyaba Mendola police station.

19

On August 4, the four of us—Pastor Hassan, Pastor Kuwa, Monim, and I—were taken to a prison cell near the court building in Khartoum for the Sudanese Attorney General to argue on our behalf concerning our poor conditions at Niyaba Mendola police station. He supervised all prosecutors in Sudan, including those who only dealt with cases referred to them from the NISS prison. Fellow prisoners had told me that he did not like the prosecutors related to NISS who were doing everything exactly as the NISS interrogators had ordered. Three hours later, the judge made his decision, and we were transferred to the more lenient, low-security Omdurman Men's Prison.

When we arrived, we saw it was divided into two sections. The "Colombia" section, as it was called, was made up of about one thousand drug dealers, drunkards, and thieves who were forced to sleep outside in large hangars without ceilings. When it rained, the dust turned to mud and flooded the hangars and everyone in them.

The smaller "VIP" section was reserved for about three hundred prisoners who, for the most part, had been caught cheating on their finances by writing bad checks. These prisoners received special privileges. They were allowed to sleep on metal beds and mattresses, and they were given plastic chairs instead of overturned buckets to sit on outside. The four of us were placed in this smaller section. Some of the other prisoners informed us that Muslim spies were everywhere. We suspected this, too, because fellow prisoners suspiciously watched us, monitoring us as we went about our day.

Our health was deteriorating. In addition to blistering sunburns from being held in open-air hangars, Pastor Hassan was suffering with duodenal ulcers, and Pastor Kuwa was recovering from a recent battle with malaria. I dreamed of using carbolic soap for the skin infection I contracted at the police station after washing the feces-riddled water bucket, but unfortunately, carbolic soap wasn't available in this new prison. The guards had given us all of our medicines, seemingly unconcerned with what we might have done with that many pills, but the constant dust, mud, sweat, and overall poor hygiene were affecting us all, and the August sun was unbearable.

The youth group from Pastor Hassan's church brought the four of us plastic chairs, and Hassan managed to find a metal bed for me for 250 Sudanese pounds (about $40). The bed was supposed to come with a mattress, but it didn't. Even without a mattress, I found it more bearable to sleep on the uncomfortable metal wire than on the dirty soil. We saw rats scurrying among the sleeping prisoners, looking for any signs of food in our bags.

Two days later, the youth group from Pastor Hassan's church brought three metal beds for my colleagues and four mattresses. At last we all could enjoy a comfortable bed! At night, my Sudanese brothers and I carried our beds outside to sleep under the open sky, away from our tight quarters.

There was a small chapel in the Colombia section, about three hundred feet away, which the Sudanese brothers and I were allowed to visit. It was the first chapel I had visited in months, and the other prisoners even allowed me to preach in it twice.

I I I I I I

By Saturday, August 6, I had spent two days in the Omdurman Men's prison, and I had watched other prisoners using cell phones to call their family members back home. My Sudanese fellow prisoners acquired contraband cell phones, and I used my remaining Sudanese money to buy a credit on their phone and place a call. Since my children changed their cell phone numbers frequently, I dialed the only number I could remember.

Aside from my seconds-long, scripted phone call a week and a half after my arrest and the thirty-second call from Mr. Sláma's phone when the prosecutor stepped away, the last time I had spoken to Vanda at any length was eight months earlier when I called her via Skype from the Paradise Hotel just before leaving for the Khartoum airport. To hear her voice again and to know she was okay would be nothing short of a miraculous gift from God.

I dialed the number, and the phone rang. Back in the Czech Republic, it was Saturday evening, and Vanda was in the midst of a conversation with our son. Suddenly, a strange phone number appeared on her cell phone. She immediately recognized the country code as belonging to Sudan. *Who could this be?* she wondered. *Is it the Sudanese Security?* Vanda answered the call, uncertainty filling her voice. "Hello?"

"It's me, Petr!" I blurted, my voice quivering.

Vanda's heart surged, threatening to burst through her chest. "Are you released?" she asked, her breathy question full of hope.

"No, I'm in the Omdurman prison and am able to use a friend's cell phone secretly." I didn't know how long my purchased credit would last, so I tried to get as much information about my family as possible, but Vanda desperately craved information about me. I hurriedly told her about my experiences, my journey, and how I knew God had a purpose for keeping me in prison so long. I listened to her words, the love in her voice, the ease with which we talked, and I felt like I used to when I traveled to Africa on ordinary trips. I felt as if nothing had changed and that soon I'd be coming home to meet her outside of the airport's baggage claim.

My cell phone credit lasted twenty wonderful minutes, and at the end of the call, Vanda reluctantly hung up the phone. An enormous smile stretched across her face. Following our phone call, she stayed awake all night, unable to sleep, her heart and mind flooded with adrenaline, joy, and overwhelming gratitude that the Lord had remained faithful to us both through this impossible season of tribulation.

I I I I I I

On August 8, four days after we arrived, a guard approached us. "Take everything and come with me," he ordered. The four of us left behind our metal beds and the plastic chairs and followed him to a cattle truck. It would transport us to the nearby Kober prison—a high-security prison infamous for torture.

At our destination, though, we were met with surprising news. Because the warden of Kober prison knew our case was being prosecuted, he refused to admit any of us until our trials were completed. We returned to the Omdurman Men's Prison via our cattle truck and were welcomed by a barrage of sardonic laughter coming from the NISS officers. From the looks of their faces, I knew they were going to find a way to punish us for wasting their time.

I I I I I I

Three days later, on Thursday, August 11, a guard approached us once again and said, "Take all your stuff." This time, we were certain we would be transferred away from this place permanently. The NISS officers had finally decided to follow through with their punishment.

We were loaded into a cattle truck, and the guards drove us for over an hour. Soon, my fellow prisoners realized where we were heading—to Al-Huda Prison, an enormous prison complex far outside the city. Unlike my previous prisons, which housed mainly political prisoners and men charged with less serious offenses, Al-Huda detained those who had committed all kinds of crimes, including organized theft, drug dealing, child abuse, rape, and murder. At full capacity, Al-Huda could hold up to ten thousand prisoners.

I wondered what awaited us at our new home in the Sudanese desert.

20

Our driver took us deep into the desert, about an hour and a half north of Khartoum, the capital city, and northwest of Omdurman, its sister city. I looked out of the cattle truck to my right and saw the brown landscape beginning to rise into three hills—Gebu Aba Mera, Gebel Mekhiat, and Gebel Leirik. We turned left onto a dusty road that led through a large green and white security gate that took us through the entrance of the notorious desert prison.

The size of the remote Al-Huda prison was enormous. The complex was divided into many large sections, and each section was divided into subsections that each contained four cells. Each of these cells was designed to hold one hundred prisoners. I felt a knot growing in my stomach, a nervousness, as we were taken out of the vehicle and into the prison.

The four of us were placed in a crowded cell of Section 2, and we immediately began acclimating to our new environment. The floor was covered in grey and beige tiles, and a few workers were busy coating the interior walls in white paint.

In the Niyaba Mendola police station, I often wondered why I had the tremendous privilege not to do anything else other than read my Bible. The answer to that question, and my understanding that it was all part of the Lord's wonderful plan, finally came three months later, on the day I set foot in Al-Huda.

This transfer to Al-Huda had been wrought with disappointment that edged on grief. Not only had I lost the privacy of my solitary confinement cell in the Niyaba Mendola police station, but later that night, I would discover that this new cell was too dark for me to read my Bible at all. I soon learned, though, that the Lord intended something far more exciting for me here in the desert.

Two prisoners with friendly, peaceful smiles entered our crowded cell the afternoon that we arrived at Al-Huda. "Where are the pastors who were admitted to this prison today?" one of them asked. My colleagues and I raised our hands slowly, and the men walked over to greet us. What they said next nearly knocked me to the floor: they had come to invite us to the prison chapel.

"Prison chapel?" I asked, incredulously. "Is there a prison chapel?"

"Yes, there is!" came the smiling reply. I soon learned exactly how good this news truly was.

Unlike in the NISS prison or the Niyaba Mendola police station, where Muslims weren't allowed to go to the mosque, this large prison had not one but several mosques, one in each section, each serving a population of four hundred prisoners. Everyone was free to attend. Five times a day, the azaans still rang out the call to prayer. But here in Al-Huda, there were also many non-Muslims—Christians from South Sudan, primarily, but also animists who practiced traditional African religions. As a result, the prison authorities had accommodated the non-Muslim prisoners with a chapel.

The chapel was once a normal cell that housed one hundred men on the second floor of Section 5 of the prison complex. However, after the beds were removed and the walls were adorned with blue latex paint, the converted house of worship could seat nearly two hundred prisoners, and even more if everyone stood. The walls were covered with icons, religious art, and a crucifix that hung directly behind the preacher's head. There was a long, plastic-covered table at the front that functioned as both a pulpit and an altar, and there were chairs for the prisoners to sit in during the services.

The men who first invited us to the chapel, it turned out, were the elders of the prison church. When we arrived at Al-Huda, the elders summoned the regular attendees to the chapel. Traditional African drums announced our arrival, and within minutes, more than two dozen other prisoners gathered to welcome us to our first service. The elders called the two Sudanese pastors and me forward and, as in Acts 13:15, immediately made a surprising request: "Brothers, if you have any word of exhortation for the people, say it."

My Sudanese colleagues knew about my three months of private Bible study in the Niyaba Mendola police station, so they turned toward me and pointed. I opened my Bible and shared a word of the Lord from John 15:1–10. It was the passage of Jesus, the true vine, and His Father, the vinedresser.

The Lord was teaching about the process of pruning us as branches, I began. "Sometimes it hurts when the Lord is pruning our lives." I continued by telling them the story of Monica Dra from Nigeria. The Christian men present were deeply touched by this compelling story and couldn't believe their ears when I shared the response of the ISIS militants in the NISS prison.

The Lord had given me one opportunity to preach at the Omdurman Men's Prison, but it was only a foreshadowing of what God had in store for me at Al-Huda. In this wilderness, this desert prison, I had found an oasis for my body and soul.

Two days after our arrival, I was transferred from Section 2 of Al-Huda to Section 3, where some of the most dangerous men were kept. These were men like Shukwan who, ten years earlier, was sentenced to seven and a half years in prison for unintentionally killing his friend in a brawl. He was a hardened man, a fighter by nature whose body was covered in scars.

But for three years, Shukwan had been a follower of Jesus Christ, having come to know the Lord through the Christian testimonies of his fellow prisoners in Al-Huda. Even though he had completed his prison sentence for manslaughter, he had been refused release until he was able to pay his court fees of 38,000 Sudanese pounds ($6,300 according to the official exchange rate, around $2,000 by the inflation-affected street exchange rate).

The first night after my transfer, Brother Shukwan saw me sleeping on the floor and told me that he wanted to take my place. Shukwan climbed out of his bed and slept on the floor, letting me enjoy a good night's sleep in his bed. His selfless act was one of the most compelling evidences I had seen of a heart that had been softened and shaped by the love of Jesus Christ. In Al-Huda, men could wait months or even years to inherit a bed from a previous prisoner, so his offer—expecting nothing in return—was remarkable. It was also a tremendous testimony to the other Muslims in our cell. Before, they respected him because he used to be a stronger fighter, but now they respected him even more because of this act of sacrifice and love.

As incredible as Shukwan's gesture was, though, the good night's sleep did little to remove the constant concern that I could spend the rest of my life in prison.

21

Everything in Al-Huda was dirty except the chapel. We kept it exceptionally clean and even paid some of the guards extra money to fumigate it once a month to eradicate the mosquitoes. There was running water in the room, but the pressure was low and required an electric pump to push the water up and into the building. When the water was running, we always took the opportunity to fill several large barrels so we would have something to drink when the power unexpectedly went out.

The running water in the chapel allowed me to refill my four two-liter plastic jugs, which I balanced in my arms as I carried them to my cell, and there was also a bathroom there where I could bathe. Every morning at 7:00 a.m., just after morning attendance was taken, I immediately walked to the chapel to rinse my body with a bucket of water. I learned that I needed to get there quickly, especially before the other prisoners arrived, lest someone steal my belongings.

There were five church services held in our chapel each week, and Christians from all backgrounds and denominations were welcome to attend.

On Sundays, a group of Eritreans came to worship. In keeping with their tradition, they removed their shoes and kissed the pictures of Mary hanging on the wall three times. They did the same with the crucifix on the wall. My heart was heavy as I watched their traditional rituals, longing to be sure they knew the living Christ depicted in the icons and not just the rituals built up around His story.

On one occasion, I was preaching a sermon on John 3:14–15. In that passage, Jesus Christ explained to Nicodemus that, just as Moses lifted up the serpent in the wilderness, so must the Son of Man be lifted up so that whoever believes in Him may have eternal life. I mentioned the story from Numbers 21. The Israelites were wandering through the desert and were bitten by snakes. Moses was instructed to lift a bronze serpent up on a pole, and everyone who had been bitten could look to it and be healed. So it is with us, I said. When we realize that we are sinners, we need to look at Jesus, who is lifted up on the cross, to be saved. Looking to Jesus Christ is the only way to be healed and truly born again.

Then I mentioned 2 Kings 18:4, a verse the Holy Spirit reminded me of as I was struggling with all the Christian idolatry that might have been expressed by all the bowing down and kissing of the religious symbols on the chapel walls. The text talks about the Judean king Hezekiah, who removed the high places and broke the pillars and cut down the Asherah (a pole or a tree that was worshiped). And he broke in pieces the bronze serpent that Moses had made, for until those days, the people of Israel had made offerings to it (it was called *Nehushtan*). I explained to my fellow prisoners that just as the bronze snake on the pole, which was originally meant to save the lives of the Israelites, became an object of idolatry, so it is when we would rather kiss and bow before a physical replica of the cross than before Christ himself.

An amazing thing happened after my sermon: many of the Eritrean fellow prisoners came to me and expressed their thanks, saying the Holy Spirit had opened their eyes and that they would bow before Christ rather than before the crucifix and dedicate their lives to Him.

Most of the Eritreans were in prison because they had entered Sudan illegally with hopes of traveling first to Libya and then on to Europe. This crime was punished by requiring the convicted to pay four thousand Sudanese pounds or by putting him in prison for three months. Many were released quickly because their relatives paid the ransom, but others served the full sentence.

Since I had arrived, the Lord had been faithful in allowing me to preach in the chapel worship services once every week and sometimes even twice a week. Knowing how many non-believers came to our services, the majority of my sermons were evangelistic, but every third sermon or so was geared toward fellow believers in Christ. I used these sermons to prepare them for persecution.

In these messages, I preached the "persecution gospel"—the message that we follow a suffering Savior who allows us to suffer as well. Jesus Christ died on the cross, enduring unspeakable cruelty so that Christians could escape the bondage of sin and death and live eternally. As His followers, we, too, will suffer here on earth. And when we suffer for our faith, we partake in the suffering of Christ. I shared stories of Christian persecution, more stories of women like Monica and boys like Danjuma, and did my best to prepare the men of Al-Huda to experience persecution and to understand it in light of Scripture.

This persecution gospel, I believe, is the true Gospel of Jesus Christ.

| | | | | | |

The chapel services began the same way, at 9:00 a.m. five times per week, with the ringing of a bell. Before the prayer time and sermon, there was always worship music. The prisoners sang traditional African songs in Arabic, and instead of playing guitars or other Western instruments, they used African instruments like maracas and bongo drums. They created the drums themselves during Eid al-Adha, the Muslim "Festival of Sacrifice."

As part of the widely celebrated festival, each cell in the prison was given a slaughtered ram. Some of the Christians at Al-Huda refused to eat the meat since they believed the New Testament forbids eating flesh offered to idols (1 Corinthians 8). I chose to follow the apostle Paul's explanation that we can eat whatever is sold in the meat market without raising any question on the ground of conscience because "the earth is the Lord's, and the fullness thereof" (1 Corinthians 10:25–26). Therefore, to me, this meat was a gift from the Lord, and I enjoyed eating every gram of its delicious protein.

Every part of the ram was used to make something. Some of the prisoners brought the ram skins to our chapel to make the drums we used in worship. Tanning leather was an elaborate process. For three weeks, the skin was soaked in sodium hydroxide, which gave off a gut-wrenching smell but dissolved all the fat, meat, and other remnants from the skin. After that, the prisoners washed, cut, and dried the skin in the sun before stretching and attaching it to the drums.

The worship began as a few soft voices from a small group of Christians who begin singing and playing drums. Soon, other prisoners heard them singing and joined in. The sound grew louder and louder, organically spreading from cell to cell and from section to section until Christians from across the entire prison were praising God together and coming to the chapel to worship.

At Al-Huda, this was the Christian answer to the Muslim call to prayer.

| | | | | | |

We sometimes had a Catholic priest who led mass and administered the Eucharist. Occasionally, we also had an Orthodox priest who conducted a very traditional mass for the Orthodox Sudanese Christians. We also had preachers who came from charismatic backgrounds. These men prayed for miraculous healings among the prisoners, and they even cast out demons, a common occurrence in this part of Africa.

The two Sudanese pastors imprisoned with me were among the rotating preachers. They were part of a healthy church denomination in Sudan, and their sermons were very Bible-based. I usually preached on Fridays and Sundays—and on any other day I was assigned. No matter our background or Christian tradition, all of us centered our sermons on the core elements of the Gospel, the importance of the Bible, and what it means to be born again.

One Friday, I was preaching about the man who was born blind in John 9. At the conclusion of the service, I gave attendees an opportunity to respond publicly to God's prompting. Anyone who wanted to begin his journey of faith with Jesus Christ was invited to come to the front of the chapel. That day, by God's grace, twelve men stood to their feet and came forward. Each week, God continued to amaze us with how many lives He was changing.

Not every prisoner who came to our chapel, though, was a Christian. We welcomed men from South Sudan also, men who worshipped animals and practiced all kinds of traditional African religions. My heart really hurt for them, and I tried my best to tailor my sermons to them with hope that God would use my broken words to speak directly to their hearts.

My goal in these sermons was not to disparage or criticize the prisoners' backgrounds or cultures; instead, I wanted to lead them to Jesus Christ, who said, "I am the way, and the truth, and the life. No one comes to the Father except through me" (John 14:6).

Before and after each sermon, I constantly prayed that the Holy Spirit would reveal the truth to these men and that they would know that, no matter what they had done, God loves them, forgives them, and desires a personal relationship with them. Because of God's work, many of these animists received the Gospel and came to know the Lord.

I was no longer worried about how long I had to stay in prison. As long as the Lord wanted me to be there, I would be there—not a day more or less.

| | | | | | |

At Omdurman, the Sudanese pastors had been visited three times each day by members of their family and church. Because of the remoteness of Al-Huda, though, my two friends only received guests twice each week.

Vanda wanted to visit me in prison, but the Minister of Foreign Affairs in the Czech Republic initially dissuaded her. When an organization raised money for her to visit me, the Czech government finally agreed, but I told the Czech consular officer that I didn't want my family to come to Sudan.

My son and I share the same name, and I was afraid of what might happen to them if they came.

I   I   I   I   I   I

I quickly learned that some of the worst behavior in this prison came from the Sudanese guards. Large sums of money were allocated to renovate this prison, but the guards confiscated it and divided the funds among themselves. The guards were constantly using drugs and demanding money from inmates.

From my new cellmates, I learned that at least twice each week, the electricity went out in the prison. The ceiling fans stopped, the light bulbs went dark, and the cooking equipment stopped functioning. The long-serving prisoners blamed the guards for deliberately turning off the power to generate income.

"Each cell needs to give us 100 pounds to fix the problem," the guards would say. When the prisoners gave in to their demands and paid the money, the power suddenly returned.

At 5:00 p.m., the guards took a headcount of the prisoners and then locked the cell doors. "When they lock our cells," a prisoner told me, "we have freedom." After our first night in Section 2, I understood why. When the doors locked, I saw the prisoners pull out their cell phones and begin making calls.

When the electricity shut off, the tension among inmates escalated inside our crowded cells, and many prisoners flocked to the chapel to get some fresh air and cool off. The chapel was a quiet place, and I spent my time going there to study the Bible, encourage other prisoners, and engage in lengthy conversations with men who had just become Christians or who wanted to commit to following Christ. Men were hungry for God in this prison, and the chapel was ideally suited for spiritual conversations.

22

After more than eight months in prison, the day of my trial finally arrived on Sunday, August 21, 2016. Pastor Hassan, Pastor Kuwa, Monim, and I were all co-defendants.

Early in the morning, we rinsed ourselves with the bucket of water in the chapel and then dressed for court. The two pastors wore black pants, black shirts, and clerical collars, and I chose jeans, a grey T-shirt, and slippers. My hair and beard were now long and silver, and I felt entirely unkempt as I learned that our first court hearing had finally arrived.

Special guards—the court police—transported us from Al-Huda to the prison building of the Khartoum Center. The guards removed our handcuffs for the journey from Al-Huda, which took nearly two hours in the back of a cattle truck, and we sat on long metal benches on each side of the truck bed.

When we arrived at the prison building, the guards put the handcuffs back on our wrists and moved us into a holding cell, where we waited.

There were dozens of prisoners squeezed into the small room. The floor of the waiting room was dirty, and there was no place to sit, so we roamed the adjacent outdoor courtyard, hemmed in with barbed wire, for hours. As I paced around the small space, I heard the sound of singing rising from outside the nearby courthouse.

My brothers and I soon realized the source of the singing, and we were overwhelmed. Hundreds of Christians from Pastor Kuwa's tribe in the Nuba Mountains had traveled by bus to Khartoum to show their support. With shields, batons, and tear gas, though, the Sudanese riot police had prevented them from entering the building. They stood outside and sang about David and Goliath, and as we waited in the courtyard for the first hearing, we listened as the Body of Christ raised up a song of encouragement for us. They were risking their own lives by offering such blatant support for us, and their bravery astounded me. I wondered how many of them would be arrested. Pastor Kuwa had tears in his eyes as he listened to the songs in the language of his heart.

Finally, shortly before 1:00 p.m., we were summoned into the Khartoum Center courtroom for our first hearing. Armed guards wearing blue uniforms and carrying AK-47s retrieved us from the holding cell. I was sure the four of us seemed like a motley crew; the guards had handcuffed us so that we looked like dangerous criminals. Pastor Hassan and I were chained together, as were Pastor Kuwa and Monim, and as we walked from the courtyard to the building, we passed the crowd of Christians from the Nuba Mountains. Hassan and I raised our hands and waved, and the crowd erupted in cheers. I didn't understand their words, but the tears in Hassan and Kuwa's eyes told me everything I needed to know. The sound of their voices followed us from the holding cell to the building, and I struggled to contain my emotion.

Soon, we arrived at the courtroom. It was a decrepit, neglected space with pale yellow plaster falling off the walls, and it smelled of mold. Someone had opened the windows, which were aluminum with dirty and broken panes, and the breeze made the smell and the heat a bit more bearable, though not enough to keep me from sweating.

As we walked into the room, I saw the security presence was heightened inside as well. In addition to the NISS officers, court police, and prison police, there were heavily armed men wearing riot gear and carrying tear gas. In addition to the Christians outside, a large group of supporters was now inside the building as well. Some were members of local churches, Hassan and Kuwa told me. Others, I came to find out, were undercover representatives of a human rights organization established to promote voting rights and democratic systems in Sudan. I had met some members of this organization among my fellow prisoners. I also saw representatives from the US Embassy and the Swiss Consulate, along with the Czech consular officer and a representative connected to the International Criminal Court. Near them were other men and women in professional clothing who appeared to be diplomats from other European countries and the European Union. They filled all of the available seats and spilled onto the floor.

Three months earlier, the NISS had finally opened case number 41/2016, but it wasn't until August, when we were transferred to Omdurman Prison and then to Al-Huda, that the case was actually referred to the court. The first court hearing was originally scheduled for the previous Sunday, but it was postponed. The guards claimed this was because rain prevented us from being transported from the prison to the court, but we soon learned the real reason. When the NISS saw the massive presence of the Christians from the Nuba Mountains—men and women who had arrived in Khartoum after an arduous, days-long journey in very uncomfortable buses—they postponed our hearing with the expectation that the Nuba believers would soon return home. However, the Christians had no intention of leaving without showing their support for their pastors. Determined to stay until the postponed first hearing, they were welcomed into the homes of other Christians in Khartoum, and they waited.

It was now shortly after 1:00 p.m. on August 21, and our trial was finally beginning. The presiding judge was Justice Dr. Osama

Mohammed Abdalla, and he sat on an elevated platform at the front of the courtroom, wearing a black robe. Abdurrahman Ahmed Abdurrahman was the investigating counsel, and more than a dozen attorneys—three official lawyers and as many as fourteen volunteers from various human rights organizations—had appeared to represent the four of us. There were so many that the court assistants had to add additional chairs to the lawyers' bench.

My personal attorney, Dr. Shumayna, had been recommended by the Czech Embassy, but I suspected he was sympathetic to the NISS, so I didn't trust him. He was eighty-four years old, dressed in an expensive suit, and had demanded an extremely steep retainer fee, possibly for bribing officials in the corrupt Sudanese legal system. He appeared to be well respected by the prosecutors and had quite a bit of clout with the officers at the Niyaba Mendola police station, where I first met him. However, he had also failed to meet me at Al-Huda for a scheduled meeting to discuss the case just before the first court hearing simply because he considered it too far of a drive. This was a tremendous blow to my confidence in him and to my morale.

The court hearing was conducted entirely in Arabic. In addition to a row of journalists and a smattering of human rights defenders, the rest of the courtroom was packed with courageous Christians who came to support us with their presence. Family members of my Sudanese fellow prisoners were crowded in seats near the front of the courtroom.

Finally, the hearing began.

"On December 18," Mr. Abdurrahman explained, "the NISS arrested a group of Christian pastors and other leaders. All of those men have been released except for the four defendants present here today. They were arrested for attending the Sudanese and South Sudanese Christian conference in Addis Ababa in October of 2015."

Mr. Abdurrahman read the list of charges under Articles 21, 50, 51, 53, 57, 64 and 66 of the Sudan Criminal Penal Code of 1991,

Article 30-1 of the Nationality Act, and Article 23 of the Regulation of Humanitarian Voluntary Work. The charges against me were extensive: joint acts in execution of criminal conspiracy, undermining the constitutional system, waging war against the state, espionage against the country, entering and photographing military areas and works, provoking hatred against or amongst sects, publication of false news, illegally entering Sudan, and running activities for charity organizations without a license.

According to the investigating counsel, we had been accused of carrying out intelligence activities against Sudan and giving tangible support to the Sudan People's Liberation Army in the Nuba Mountains. He explained that we had worked to compile evidence that supported various allegations against the Sudanese government: acts of violence, including civilian displacement, extrajudicial killings, burning villages, and genocide; the oppression and torture of Christians; and the demolition of churches.

I did not trust the translator, who had been supplied by the NISS. His mastery of English was woefully inadequate, which first became obvious to me when he translated that I came to Sudan on a "*terrorist* visa" instead of a "*tourist* visa." My Sudanese brothers, who sat on the bench next to me, confirmed my suspicions: he wasn't translating accurately at all. They tried to object, but the judge silenced them.

Our attorneys denied the charges against us, and court was adjourned until August 29. We complained to our lawyers about the translator, and then Pastor Hassan, Pastor Kuwa, Monim, and I were handcuffed in pairs and escorted from the courtroom and back into the prison building waiting room. After several more hours, we climbed once again into the cattle truck and began the journey back to our desert prison.

The charges levied against me were staggering, but I wasn't worried. I knew the Supreme Judge, and He doesn't wear a black robe.

| | | | | | |

Cell phones could be purchased illegally after being smuggled into prison, and Monim bought one. He let me use it to call my family every day for about an hour. I purchased a SIM card and asked my fellow prisoners to recharge it with a new credit whenever needed. My family decided to send me a simple cell phone through the consular officer. At the next hearing, I received a plastic bag with some toiletries, dried food—and the most important thing: the cell phone with some important numbers saved in its memory. Nobody at the courthouse bothered to search us because they knew we would be carefully searched before entering Al-Huda. So the problem was how to smuggle the phone into the prison.

On the way from the first court hearing in central Khartoum, we asked our accompanying guards to stop at a bakery so we could purchase a few loaves of round bread packed in two plastic bags. For a small bribe, the guards were happy to stop.

My more experienced fellow prisoners taught me how to slide the phone and its charger into the breads in the middle of the plastic bag. That way, when the guards searched the bags of bread, they would only touch the four sides and leave the middle unexamined.

The plan worked brilliantly. I opened the bread, took out the cell phone, and waited for the cell doors to lock. Finally, I was able to call my family. I was so relieved to have this regular contact with Vanda, Váva, and Petr, and I used the time to encourage them with the truths God was revealing to me through His Word.

At 6:00 a.m. each morning, the cell doors unlocked, and our cell phones slid into the secret hiding places where they would remain until night fell again. At first, I carried my phone with me, but when a guard stopped me for a surprise search and found my cell phone on me, he charged me fifty Sudanese pounds to get it back. After that, each morning before we lined up for morning attendance, I gave my phone to Shukwan. He locked it in a wooden box that he stored under my bed, and I knew it would be safe until night. After morning attendance, we were permitted to roam throughout our section of the prison complex without restrictions, and I spent most of my time in the chapel.

I   I   I   I   I   I

In my previous prisons, sending and receiving letters was a laborious, lengthy task, and the letters were censored. This prevented me from being completely transparent in my letters—I wrote in English, they were checked by the Secret Police, and it took quite some time for them to be delivered through visits by the consular officer.

But now, in Al-Huda, we had access to smartphones. I quickly realized that I could write a letter in Czech, photograph each page with the phone's camera, and send the complete letter to my daughter's cell phone via an encrypted application called WhatsApp.

A week after our first court hearing and a day before the second, I wrote my first secret letter in Czech to my family. In it, I compared the limited time of suffering in prison with the eternal life of the men in Al-Huda who were followers of Jesus Christ. I gave thanks for Brother Shukwan, my cellmate whom I referred to in coded language as my "guardian angel." Shukwan had been preparing and enhancing the pitiful prison food and allowing me to gain back some of the weight I had lost, and I told my family how he asked me to bless our meals in front of our Muslim cellmates. This had allowed me to phrase my prayers as short sermons in English for those who could understand.

Often, I witnessed Shukwan reading the gospels from his Arabic New Testament, and the Muslim prisoners in our corner of the cell asked him questions about the truth of the Bible. Shukwan proved an effective apologist and answered their objections well. Each time he shared the Gospel with the Muslims, I prayed silently for him.

At the end of my letter, I shared how I was reassured that I would stay in prison only as long as the Lord wanted to use me there. When

I was finished writing, my letter was eight pages long, and it felt wonderful to finally be able to write so freely to my wife and children.

There was a second benefit to having smartphones in Al-Huda. From Hassan's phone, on extremely slow 2G internet in the middle of the Sudanese desert, we were able to see people around the world throwing more and more support our way. CitizenGo, a human rights organization that campaigns on behalf of persecuted people, began an online petition for us. Huddled around Hassan's phone, we refreshed the website over and over again, watching in awe as the number of signatures increased. We each signed the petition ourselves, and every morning, someone new in our prison would pull us aside and tell us that he, too, had signed our petition. We monitored the petition daily, and were amazed when the number of signatures peaked at nearly half a million.

On another occasion, someone told us there was a YouTube video of a peaceful demonstration in front of the Sudanese Embassy in Madrid, Spain. Even though the video played intermittently on our unreliable internet connection, I was moved and incredibly encouraged to see posters with my own name on them and to hear people shouting for me. In the twenty-minute video, the camera panned across the crowd, moving from sign to sign, from banner to banner, each demanding freedom for Petr Jašek.

I   I   I   I   I   I

A week after our first hearing, we began our second journey to the Khartoum Center courtroom for another. As before, we waited in the small, dirty cell for two and a half hours before the 1:00 p.m. hearing began. A dozen children were with us in the cell—children who had grown up in squalor and had become thieves—and when the pastors' families brought us food, we shared it with them. The youngest child was nine years old.

As the hearing began, I saw that the investigating counsel—the man who had conducted the investigation into our crimes and who now led our prosecution—had set up a projector in the courtroom. On it, he began to splash the photos the NISS had recovered from my hard drive: photos of the destroyed Christian churches in the north and those taken in the Nuba Mountain war zone.

As I watched the photos flash across the screen, my eyes gravitated toward a small detail in the corner: the date was stamped digitally on the photos as 2011. I sat up straight on the bench and drew a quick breath, adrenaline surging through my veins. *Finally, proof that I am innocent of this charge!* I leaned to my lawyer and whispered, "These are not my photos. I was not there in 2011!" The prosecutor objected to my speaking with my lawyer in English, and the judge agreed. Loud arguments ensued between the lawyers and the judge.

But moments later, the electricity in the building went out, and the investigating counsel's projector was plunged into darkness. Most of the people present in the courtroom burst into laughter; losing power was a daily experience for the Sudanese people, and only the wealthiest could afford to have a generator. Without electricity in the building, court was adjourned until September 1. We had been in the courtroom for only twenty minutes, but I could see that the Sudanese Security planned to seize any chance to delay our hearings. This didn't bother me as much as it might have, though, because I now had a new mission: to find evidence proving I had not visited Sudan in 2011.

23

When I returned to Al-Huda, I immediately contacted Váva and asked her to scan and email to my lawyer any documents I had proving that I had been in Prague on the date the photos that I'd seen in court that day had been taken in the Nuba Mountains. This was the evidence I would need to prove my innocence! Excitement coursed through my body with the knowledge that I would soon be exonerated.

On the morning of September 1, we again left our cells to begin the long journey to Khartoum. On our way through the Al-Huda prison, I witnessed a horrifying spectacle.

"Look to your right," I whispered, nudging Hassan and Kuwa. As we walked through the prison yard, we saw a prisoner being dipped into an open sewer filled with human feces. I felt profound empathy for him and prayed for God's protection for him as we watched the guards restrain his body until the excrement reached his neck.

From other inmates, we knew that for his serious offense—probably striking a guard—the man would be held in the sewer for at least half an hour. It was the worst punishment the guards could exact. For lesser infractions, they made prisoners roll around in the dirt outside, knowing they'd be unable to get fully clean with such limited access to running water. For more serious offenses, the guards chained the inmates' legs for one, two, or even three weeks, the heavy metal digging into their ankles. In some ways, removing the chains was even worse, since the iron chisel used to sever the lock often sliced the prisoners' skin.

The most serious punishment, though, was what we had just witnessed, and it was not an uncommon one in Al-Huda. Any time we smelled a noxious odor like one from a pig farm, we knew the lid to the sewer system had been opened and the tank was ready for another prisoner to be punished. For thirty minutes, he stood in the sewer, human feces covering his shoulders and inching up his neck. When the humiliation was over, he had a very limited ability to wash his body. It was no wonder that cholera spread rampantly throughout Al-Huda. In an effort to contain the infectious disease, prison doctors distributed three tablets of doxycycline to each healthy inmate, wrongly assuming that they could use the antibiotics as a prevention. I prayed every day that I would be spared. Tuberculosis ran rampant as well, and prison guards entered the cells periodically to remove the dead bodies from our midst.

I I I I I I

By the time our third hearing began, the translator had been dismissed. I was not particularly bothered by his removal, even though this now left me without a formal translator during the proceedings.

The sessions reminded me of trials in the 1950s in Czechoslovakia, when the Communists would arbitrarily sentence defendants they deemed ideologically threatening to a lifetime of imprisonment. Instead of worrying about my trial, I chose to praise the Lord and pray silently. Besides, the trial should be over in a few short weeks anyway.

The third hearing was another tedious and frustrating occasion on which the investigative counsel presented evidence of my meeting with the young Muslim convert to Christ whose body was burned.

Chapter Twenty-Three

My lawyer insisted on getting technical experts to test the authenticity of the materials the prosecutors presented.

Afterward, I wrote a letter to my family.

The court hearing for Europeans is very chaotic. The judge, defense lawyers, and prosecutors are shouting over each other. The Secret Service also takes part in the hearings and directs all. The judge alone is known as a member of the secret police, so we know that the verdict will be probably the same as the prosecution wants.

I and the three brothers who are also accused in the same case remain settled. We know that the Lord has all in His hands and that He is the one who will have the last and decisive word. I find great encouragement and strength in remembering Psalm 109:30–31.

Thank you very much for all verses you have sent me as encouragement for me. I see them as a great confirmation of what the Lord gives me for every day. The Lord gives me time for refreshing with Him and time for sharing the Gospel, time for spiritual self-building, and time for encouragement with and by dear brothers in Christ.

Of the nearly nine months that I have spent in prison, I have spent four months in solitary confinement. For the first five months, I was without a Bible. But the Lord spoke to me through the Holy Spirit and showed me His word through remembering known verses. Later, He gave me a new, deeper understanding for parts of the Bible that I hadn't understood in the past or that I understood incorrectly.

Thank you for your prayers and words of encouragement. Let the Lord protect you and bless you all. 1 Peter 2:20b–23

| | | | | | |

Two weeks earlier, on August 15, Vanda and our children had composed a letter and prepared a care package to send to me via the new Czech consular officer, Mr. Afifi. "I am really proud of you,"

Vanda wrote, "for your bravery and the patience with which you are able to tolerate the whole situation. You are a great example and encouragement for all of us. I am reading all your letters and keeping them in my heart!"

When I first met with Mr. Afifi following my third hearing, I was able to receive their gifts, read their letter, and send a response.

My dear ones,

Thank you very much for the money I have received through the honorary consul Mr. Afifi. I managed to carry the mobile phone to the prison, and it cost me only two small "gifts" for the guards. You can get nearly everything into Sudanese prison for money.

The greatest joy I had was from the book by Richard Wurmbrand named If Prison Walls Could Speak. *I read this book about twenty years ago, but now when I am in a similar situation as Brother Wurmbrand, this book speaks directly to my heart! Lots of situations that I live in here bring feelings very similar to Richard's. More than once, this book touched me so intensively that I was in tears. I read this book right through during one afternoon, but I really look forward to reading it once more.*

I was amazed that my prison experiences—my feelings and my theological understanding of so many passages of Scripture—were so similar to those of Richard Wurmbrand, even though our situations differed in time and place. I was imprisoned in 2016 by the totalitarian government of Sudan; he was imprisoned decades earlier by the totalitarian government of Communist Romania. But I felt an amazing connection to him in persecution. We shared a common bond, a common plight, a common Christ. If God ever released me from prison, as Wurmbrand was once released, I prayed He would also give me the courage to record my testimony so that others could come to know the love of Christ.

24

My time in Al-Huda Prison was proving to be emotionally and spiritually edifying. My family had sent an MP3 player with audio recordings in both Czech and English of the Bible, and they also sent a French textbook. I listened to Scripture late into the evening, long after the sun had set and I no longer had enough light to read, and I also used the audio recordings to teach English and French in the Al-Huda chapel room.

However, even though my mind and spirit were nourished, the weekly trips to the Khartoum courthouse were taking a toll. It was still scorchingly hot in Sudan, and the grueling journeys in the back of the cattle truck were extremely unpleasant. I began to dread our Sunday morning journeys to the Khartoum Court building.

On September 5, we arrived once again for our next court proceeding. A new translator had been appointed, this one a lecturer from Khartoum University's translation department.

Throughout the hearing, my words from the many interrogations were misrepresented and distorted. Hassan leaned toward me and whispered that I was accused of admitting that I was a representative of an American organization tasked with providing assistance to the injured young man—something I never would have confessed to. He also translated that I was being accused of giving money to overthrow the government. As the hearing continued, I watched Hassan's and

Kuwa's reactions, noticing their disappointment and frustration and hearing their frustrated murmurs.

"Objection," my lawyer said, again and again, but the judged seemed unfazed.

After the court proceeding, much of which centered on the injured Christian student, the embassy officials shook our hands and assured us that they understood that our trial was a political situation about religion. They thanked us for our patience and told us how they admired the way we were handling it.

We spent the next few hours in the holding cell, encouraged by their words. We walked among the lounging prisoners, praising the Lord for providing the support of the Nuba Christians and the embassy officials, before we were again transported back to Al-Huda.

I I I I I I

The hearings continued each week, and we made the arduous journey from Al-Huda to Khartoum again and again. Sometimes, when traffic was slow or the weather was fierce, the trip took as long as three hours. Quite often, we stopped at other court buildings in Khartoum, and our cattle truck would get so stuffed with prisoners that it was extremely difficult to breathe.

On September 26, we found ourselves again before the judge, listening to the prosecutor plead his case against us. He showed a video taken in the Nuba Mountains in 2011, and I grew excited. I knew I had evidence, provided by my family, to prove I was not even in Sudan during that time, and since much of the government's case against me hinged on the videos from the Nuba Mountains, I knew it was only a matter of time before their case against me was dismissed.

The prosecutor showed the video and the translator provided an interpretation.

"This video was found on the external hard drive of Accused #1," the prosecutor claimed, gesturing toward me. "It shows the defendant and three others in a car, driving through the Nuba Mountain war zone."

My lawyer turned to me and whispered, "Petr, they are saying that you were there on this video."

"That's obvious nonsense," I whispered back, "because I was in the Czech Republic, and I can prove it." He raised his hand to object, presumably explaining what I'd just told him, and then lifted a stack of papers from the table in front of him.

"Here is evidence that Mr. Jašek was in Prague when the video was taken." He passed copies of receipts and other paperwork to the judge and then presented forensic evidence that the video wasn't even taken with my camera; my camera was a Canon Rebel XT3, but the digital fingerprint on the video showed a stamp of "Canon Rebel XTi."

His rebuttal was solid and irrefutable, but somehow, the judge appeared unconvinced. He looked at the scanned documents before setting them to the side. The judge said something back in Arabic, and my lawyer simply raised his shoulders in disagreement. My incontrovertible evidence had fallen on deaf ears.

I looked around at the courtroom—no one was even recording my lawyer's objections. The clear evidence I'd thought would set me free wouldn't even make it into the official record of my trial!

25

On October 17, we arrived again in Khartoum for our eighth court hearing. I was discouraged that the trial had lasted two months already. Through letters and secret phone calls with my family, though, I had learned that Christians around the world were praying for me, and I found great encouragement in that knowledge.

The daily prayer and fasting chain in my church in the Czech Republic had continued, and I knew they met regularly to pray together. I also knew that at the VOM chapel service every Tuesday morning, my brothers and sisters in the United States were remembering me as well. Pastor Hassan and Pastor Kuwa had told me the entire church in Sudan was praying for us, and I thought of these Christians as I walked into the Khartoum Center for the next court session.

In the hearing, Mr. Abdurrahman—the investigator and prosecutor—claimed to have a video of our nighttime meeting with the injured student, and I realized they had captured the recording with their night-vision surveillance. He also claimed to have an audio recording of me and Monim talking about the injured student's conversion to Christianity. I found this highly unlikely because

I remembered that meeting well. We were in a loud restaurant, and it would have been nearly impossible to capture any type of usable audio from my iPhone.

I was intrigued by the next portion of the hearing, a series of questions and answers between a panel of our defense attorneys and Mr. Abdurrahman. Though my attorneys had been able to prove I'd been in the Czech Republic when a ministry colleague took the most sensitive photos in 2011—which the Sudanese secret police had restored from the deleted files on my external hard drive—the judge ignored their objection. Sudan was still accusing me of entering the Nuba Mountains that year; the secret police also had restored some of the less-sensitive deleted photos I'd taken during my trip to the Nuba Mountains in 2012, on which I appeared.

"Why did you interrogate the first defendant?" my lawyer asked, referring to me.

"Because his first visit to Sudan in 2012 was illegal, and he visited many areas in the Nuba Mountains and met with rebel fighters. During that visit, he tried to confirm the allegations of oppression, torture, and forced Islamization and Arabization of Nuba people. According to my investigation of the photo evidence," Mr. Abdurrahman continued, "he provided logistical, physical, and moral support to the rebel fighters, and he submitted a report about these allegations to international institutions, particularly the head office of the first defendant's organization." I knew he was referring to VOM.

"Where are the headquarters of VOM?"

"In the USA," he responded.

"Has there been any impact by the reports submitted by VOM?"

"Yes, the reports clearly tarnished the image of Sudan internationally in political, economic, and military terms," he said.

I was astounded by this remarkable admission: the Sudanese government did not deny that it persecuted Christians, but it objected strenuously to that information being spread outside Sudan. I shook my head at the prosecutor's comment. The problem—in the minds of my accusers—wasn't their persecution of Christians but the like-lihood that this information would tarnish the country's reputation!

This line of questioning continued for some time, with Mr. Abdurrahman testifying about various illegal activities committed by Pastor Hassan, Pastor Kuwa, Monim, and me. Our lawyers argued and objected, but with little effect. Each time, the judge sided with the prosecution.

I knew my trial was a sham—the prosecutor was the same man who conducted the investigation, and none of my lawyer's evidence was having any impact on whether I was viewed as guilty or innocent. Worst of all, the judge was obviously on the side of the prosecution; when the prosecutors were cross-examined and unable to answer suf-ficiently, the judge interfered and spoke on their behalf. I knew well that the trial was proceeding just like those in Communist Czecho-slovakia and that there was little chance that the verdict would be in my favor.

| | | | | | |

Two days later, I composed another letter to my family.

Dear ones,

> *Greetings to all of you from the prison Al-Huda. I am sin-cerely thanking all of you for your tireless prayer, fasting, and support and also for your letters, from which I am receiving great encouragement and happiness. Thank you for being such a great help to me, for your prayers and petitioning for grace (2 Cor. 1:11). I believe that we will soon be praising God all together.*

> *I am reading all the letters I have received again and again and am feeling great encouragement from them, especially from*

the Bible verses that you have sent. Thanks to your prayers, I am experiencing outstanding touches of God's hand. The strength I receive from your prayers is helping me continue in this fight of faith. God is giving me strength in my weakness (2 Cor. 12:10), and He will be the One who finishes this fight instead of me (Psalm 57:3).

Today, Paul's words have spoken to me especially strongly in 2 Corinthians 6:3, and especially in verse 10. It is only with thankfulness that I can explain the amazing joy that the Lord fills me with despite this enduring imprisonment. The longer I'm in prison, the greater my joy grows, and from Jesus's nail-pierced hand, I am experiencing new touches. All of this we can explain only by the sacrifice of Jesus Christ who has loved us. I am living, knowing, and feeling the tremendous protection and intervention from God's hands, especially whenever there is danger.

I also described in the letter a remarkable situation that had just happened there in Al-Huda—a recent and unbelievable intervention by the Lord on my behalf. Two weeks earlier, yet another dangerous prisoner had been transferred to our already-overcrowded room of about ninety-five people. There were only seventy-five beds in our cell. I learned from Brother Shukwan that the new prisoner was a drug boss who had been convicted of a crime as a teenager and was currently serving the fourteenth year of a twenty-year prison sentence. To my surprise, the man came over and sat in a bed just next to me and began distributing "bango," a hallucinogenic drug, to the other prisoners. He brought over an enormous modern television and a DVD player with hopes of transforming our quiet corner of the cell into a noisy drug den where the prisoners could smoke and watch a filmed fight.

Brother Shukwan, my "bodyguard," was outraged, and the next day, he rotated our triple-decker bed about ninety degrees to block off the corner of the cell and prevent more prisoners from coming over and watching the film. The drug boss was furious, and he didn't give up so easily. He corralled more of his friends to smoke next to my bed. On two occasions, I stood up to them directly and told them, in broken Arabic, that I strongly disagreed with their practice and that they should leave. To my surprise, the prisoners seemed to respect me and soon left the corner to smoke bango at the other end of the room.

The drug boss was now losing customers and decided to seek revenge. It was common knowledge that anyone selling drugs in this prison was always close friends with the guards, so the next day, as I walked back to my room from the chapel, some of the guards unexpectedly stopped to search me. After thoroughly rummaging through my clothes, one of them discovered my secret waist belt inside my underwear where I kept my money and mobile phone. He took my phone, which he threatened to keep unless I immediately "bought" it back for fifty Sudanese pounds (about $8).

After being harassed for several more minutes, I finally returned to our room. Everyone seemed to be expecting me, particularly the drug boss who was sitting with his arms folded across his chest, trying to intimidate me. He mocked me to my face for the rest of the afternoon, and in the evening, he placed the television right next to my legs and cranked the volume all the way up so the whole room could hear the female boxing match.

The next night, he blared the music directly into my ear until two o'clock in the morning. Miraculously, the Lord gave me enough peace and mercy to sleep through all the commotion. The other prisoners were annoyed by the incessantly loud night music and resented the drug boss, but nobody dared to confront him. I watched the attitudes of the prisoners change to hate, but I felt something else instead of hate for the man; instead, I felt sympathy. The Lord gave me a supernatural love for him, especially after reading Zechariah 4:6, a verse that spoke very powerfully to me: "Not by might, nor by power, but by my Spirit, says the Lord of hosts."

As I thought about that verse and about the man, the Holy Spirit warmed my heart. I tried to see him as Christ saw him, with love. After all, what kind of life must he have known? The man had been living at this prison for fourteen long years, ever since he was a teenager. After that, in everything I did or said, I became determined to trade kindness for his cruelty.

The next night was mysteriously calm. There was no loud music, no intimidation, harassment, or unexpected body searches by the prison guards. The biggest shock came that afternoon when I returned from the chapel to discover that the drug boss's bed was empty. The television and DVD player were gone as well. After asking what happened, I learned that the man was suddenly and inexplicably transferred to another Sudanese prison approximately six hundred miles away. I couldn't believe the news and spent the night praying for him, asking God to show him mercy. The swiftness of the Lord's intervention in this situation, however, reminded me that even in this cell, as I was surrounded by criminals, murderers, thieves, and drug dealers, God was watching over me, protecting me, preserving me, and reminding me that I belong to Him. As Zechariah 2:8 says, "He who touches you touches the apple of his eye."

26

For the next two weeks, our court hearings were postponed, and we waited anxiously for any news or updates. On November 3, we finally returned to Khartoum and discovered that the prosecution had rested its case. It was now time for our defense to present ours.

My lawyer began his cross examination of the prosecutor. His bravery in standing up to the government was astounding. Even thinking back on it now fills my heart with gratitude.

"Is there any condition in issuing Sudanese visas that prevents the visitor from meeting Sudanese people?" he asked. "Is there any kind of war between Sudan and the Czech Republic?"

No, Mr. Abdurrahman answered.

"According to your investigation, most of these photos were taken in 2011 in the Nuba Mountains. Was Mr. Jašek even there?"

The questions continued, with my lawyer discrediting the audio, video, and photographic evidence that the prosecution presented.

"Did you carry out a voice comparison? Do you know that voices can be tampered with using technology? The camera brought as an exhibit—was it the same camera used in taking the photographs?"

Mr. Abdurrahman admitted that I was not present in 2011, but he found the photos dated 2012 sufficiently damning, despite the fact that they were clearly taken with a different model of Canon camera.

Our lawyers continued their questioning by focusing on the conference in Addis Ababa, the photos of the injured student, and the humanitarian aid offered to him. Mr. Abdurrahman conceded to nearly all of the defense's arguments, and I began to see a glimmer of hope.

It took the prosecution three months to present their case against us, but it took only three hours for our attorneys to completely dismantle it.

I I I I I I

My hope did not last long. Over the months of November and December, we had seven more weekly hearings, and it became clear to me that despite the many inaccuracies in the state's case, they had much evidence against me. The prosecution argued that I had conducted hostile activity against the state that threatened the country's national and social security. The "illegal humanitarian work" I conducted supposedly threatened national security and harmed the interests of Sudanese society. The Sudanese government was attempting to show that they had a democratic process, but I knew that regardless of any evidence my lawyers presented, the court would do whatever it wanted to do. The judge would make his ruling at the instruction of the NISS, not based on the facts of the case.

After each hearing, the pro-government newspapers published articles presenting the four of us as the worst possible criminals and the most dangerous enemies of the Sudanese government. Even though I had seen this same practice in totalitarian countries around the world and had supported persecuted Christians in similar situations through my work, I was extremely frustrated by the injustice of the system and the helplessness I felt. I knew that I would be found guilty and that I might be sentenced to death. At the very least, I might be faced with spending the next two decades of my life in prison. At night, when I was able to talk safely by phone, I called my family and prepared them for what I knew might come. It was possible that I would be released, but I also knew that I could be sentenced to years in prison, life in prison, or even death. I wanted them to be prepared.

Consular officers and sometimes even the Czech ambassador from Cairo had been present at many of the court hearings, and they assured me they would begin negotiations for my release as soon as the verdict was announced. But would that negotiation process take weeks? Months?

"I suspect the court will sentence me to twenty years," I told the Czech consular officer one day after the court proceedings concluded.

"No, no," he said. "In these cases, they will likely sentence you to the time you have already served. I am confident you will be released."

I prayed he was correct.

27

When I was first arrested in Khartoum, I was clean-shaven and bald. Now, some eight months later, my hair had grown long in the back, and a beard now flowed from my chin and covered my neck. This was, indeed, a wilderness experience, and I felt like I looked the part—completely wild.

To prepare our own food in Al-Huda, often without electricity, we had to get creative. Burning charcoal was never the best option because the smoke would fill the cells. Even when we lit the charcoal near the door, it became nearly impossible to breathe. To offset the nauseating fumes, someone had the idea of roasting green coffee beans on a hot plate over the fire, which gave off a pleasant aroma.

The charcoal fires, though, did not provide an ideal solution to our cooking dilemma. Since the prisoners were resourceful, they managed to smuggle in all sorts of items to sell to the other inmates, so it was possible to buy just about everything. My cellmates and I purchased resistor wires to create our own electric cookers: African hotplates, as they were called. A tremendous surge of electricity hit me when I accidently touched the two live wires together, but we were eventually able to run the electric current through the resistor wires directly into several hardened, round, clay patties, which we used to heat our dinner.

I was constantly worried about someone taking my belongings. In my previous prisons, the guards always locked my carry-on suitcase in storage rooms, but here at Al-Huda, theft was common. Every prisoner was responsible for securing his own possessions. Three days after I arrived, I learned this lesson the hard way when I realized that items were disappearing from my suitcase. My deodorant, soap, food, and medicine—all of them were gone. For that reason, I started carrying my luggage with me wherever I went.

To protect my more sensitive belongings like my cell phone, credit cards, wallet, and money, I concealed them inside the secret pouch that Vanda attached to the belt around my waist. The only time the pouch ever left my body was when I removed my clothes to bathe in the prison toilet.

About one week after arriving at Al-Huda prison, I made the mistake of placing that pouch on a hanger in the bathroom. I closed my eyes for a few seconds to rinse the soap from my face, and when I opened them again, I saw that all my belongings were gone—everything. Someone had been waiting for me in the next toilet section and timed the robbery perfectly, just as I closed my eyes. The robbery left me feeling frustrated, violated and extremely angry. In a panic, I borrowed a cell phone and contacted my family with instructions to call the bank and cancel my credit cards.

A few minutes later, and to my great astonishment, Brother Shukwan walked up to me with my credit cards in his hand. Apparently, he had used his influence and forceful reputation among the prisoners to track down the thief and retrieve my phone and other valuables. The money in my wallet, however, I never saw again.

One day, I told the chapel leader that my medicine had been stolen out of my suitcase. "Bring your suitcase here," he said. "Why didn't you say so earlier?" I followed him into the chapel as he explained that only two of the five toilets were still operative, and the other three rooms were kept under lock and key because he and the elders used them for storage. He told me I could place my suitcase there whenever I needed to, and he assured me it would be safely locked.

As we approached the month of December, the daily outdoor roll call became bitterly cold. The large crowd of prisoners, sitting in rows of five, was usually silent. For most of us, mornings were the saddest moments in prison. Shivering in the darkness and cold, we all thought about our future. *Another day behind bars!* we lamented. *How many more days will we have to be here?*

Right in front of our row were three large, empty clay containers of drinking water called *dabangas*. I studied them and decided to make the most of these miserable, early morning hours by beginning my day with prayer. The dabangas, I decided, would help me still my mind and visualize my family. The first *dabanga* would be my wife, the second my daughter, and the third my son, and I would pray for them individually. After I prayed for my family, I talked to them. *Oh, my dear* dabanga *Vanda, how much longer will I have to sit here in the morning? When will I be able to wrap you in a tight embrace again?* The clear early-morning sky was full of bright stars, and I looked up and saw the moon and the Great Bear constellation. *Is Vanda looking at the same stars at this moment?* I wondered. *What is she doing right now?* In those precious moments, as I stared up at the stars, I was connected to her.

Months later, after I was released from prison and finally returned home, Vanda told me that she, too, felt connected to me through prayer during the early morning hours as she stood in the cold at the bus stop and looked at the stars.

After each morning count, I hurried to the prison chapel. My heart rejoiced as I headed up the stairs to the chapel floor, anticipating the new things my Lord had prepared for me each day. The homesickness and intense desire for my dear ones soon dissolved in the joy of the Lord.

When I wasn't ministering to prisoners, I spent my time letting God minister to me through His Word. I still had the Bible the consular officer of the Czech Embassy in Cairo had given me, and there were also Good News Bible translations here since Prison Fellowship, a worldwide organization, came occasionally to preach in Sudan. We received occasional visits from Prison Fellowship pastors, and they sometimes brought fruit and other foods to supplement our meals. Their visits offered balm to our souls and stomachs.

Our prison ministry was fruitful as well. One afternoon, Pastor Hassan and Pastor Kuwa and I were sitting in the chapel and felt a sudden, strong assurance of the Lord's purpose in our being there and preaching the Gospel to our fellow prisoners, who were utterly hopeless, desperate, and forgotten. These lost men could hear the Gospel and find reconciliation with God through the precious blood of the Lord Jesus and spend eternity in Heaven. What was one year, or possibly even more, in this agonizing situation compared with eternity in Heaven for someone who became a believer through our ministry? Hassan and Kuwa thought particularly of the prisoners on death row. We were all reminded that God's thoughts and ways are much higher than our human thoughts and ways (Isaiah 55:8–10) and that His plans are bigger than our plans.

I I I I I I

The more emotionally depleted I felt, the more the Lord lifted me up through the restorative power of His Word, through the healing presence of His Spirit, and through the ministry He allowed me to have in the Al-Huda prison chapel. I also knew that my church back home in the Czech Republic was praying and fasting regularly for me. I had not been forgotten by them, and I had not been forgotten by God. I found myself right in the Lord's will and purpose.

On my most challenging days, God proved Himself faithful in giving me just enough strength to make it to the next morning. He reminded me of 1 Peter 3:15, a verse I tried daily to practice when speaking with Muslim prisoners as well as guards: "Always being prepared to make a defense to anyone who asks you for a reason for the hope that is in you; yet do it with gentleness and respect."

Through unexpected and mysterious ways, the Lord gave me everything I needed to keep going, to keep preaching. At times, God even gave new thoughts to me, messages that I wrote down and preached in the chapel.

For some time, I had sensed that God had a purpose for putting me through this whole ordeal. Only in Al-Huda, however, had that purpose become absolutely clear. I could finally see that the Lord had been orchestrating every step of my imprisonment, from my arrest at the airport to my interrogations and isolation. He had prepared and equipped me to be His minister to these prisoners at Al-Huda.

In the first five months of my imprisonment, when I was without my Bible, my prayer life deepened tremendously. Then, during my three months with a Bible in solitary confinement, I had an opportunity for much in-depth study. I made hundreds of notes from my readings—literally filling the margins of each page and the empty spaces in the front matter of my Bible with tiny, carefully lettered notes. Many of these became sermons, and this time of special, deep Bible study equipped me to preach during the following six months of prison ministry in the Al-Huda chapel. The Lord gave me an abundance of material to use, and even though I had not preached many sermons in English, I trusted that God would always give me the right words to say.

I was determined to seize every opportunity to share the Gospel.

28

I had been in Sudanese captivity for just over one year, and even though I was able to talk to my family by phone nearly every night, I marked the occasion by writing a letter to them.

"Dear ones," I penned, "Greetings to all of you and abundance of wishes for God's peace at this season of Advent!"

I thanked them for their prayers, fasting, and encouraging letters—and especially for including the Bible verses—spiritual reminders that always brought me so much pleasure. I let them know that God had answered their prayers, that He was filling me and my prisonmates with tremendous joy and heavenly peace. Humanly speaking, the uneasy year had been marked by countless atrocities, crimes, acts of torture, and inhuman cruelty. Still, the Lord was filling my mind with the sureness of His eternal purpose. God had a plan for me—I knew this without doubt. And on this anniversary, I was all the more confident that every hour that had passed and every minute I had spent in all the various prisons throughout Sudan wasn't without meaning. God wastes nothing.

I lifted my hand from the page and paused to reflect on how the Lord had refined and shaped me through the last twelve months of captivity. In many ways, I felt like Joseph in the Old Testament, who was falsely accused and imprisoned in Egypt. His feet were bruised with shackles. The jailers placed iron chains around his neck. But the Psalmist was right: "The word of the Lord tested him" (Psalm 105:19).

Every day, I prayed for strength to pass this great test, to endure the suffering, and to prove myself worthy of the burden that God had graciously placed on my shoulders. It astounded me to think that God had decided to use *me* to share His amazing plan of salvation and to do His life-saving work in these prisons—work that He had prepared before the creation of this world. Even though my living conditions were getting worse and worse and even though each new prison brought new challenges and tribulations, God was giving me small glimpses of His master plan and providential will. In my darkest moments, Jesus continued to be my light and life.

When I thought back to December 10, 2015, and how I was arrested at the airport, about the nearly four months in the NISS prison, and about being moved to the police station in Niyaba Mendola, my heart flooded to the brim with gratitude. During those first four horrendous months when I received only sporadic information from home, I repeatedly asked the Lord a simple question: *How long will I have to endure this prison before I will see my family again?* God didn't answer my question on that day, April 10, when already four long months in prison had passed; instead, He waited until the next day when twelve emigrants from Eritrea, arrested at the Libyan border, walked into our overcrowded room. That evening, the voice of the Savior was loud and clear: *Go and share the Gospel with them!*

"So I gave them my testimony," I continued writing in the letter to my family. I told them that even though I had grown up in a Christian home, a time came when I had to make the most important decision of my life: not only to invite Jesus Christ into my life, but also to ask Him to take control of it. These men were refugees who had tried to escape from the post-Communist, totalitarian Eritrea where the president persecuted religious minorities. I told them I also had tried to escape Communist Czechoslovakia in 1988 when the borders inched open, but I ultimately couldn't leave because I felt that it wasn't the Lord's will for my life. I told them about my later attempts to escape Communism and expressed that when a person commits his life into the Lord's hands, He takes care of that person and provides the best possible future.

We talked all night, and, almost with tears in my eyes, I invited my new Eritrean friends to reach out and touch the nail-pierced hands of Christ—hands that are outstretched to everyone in the world. Those hands belong to the One who gave His life for us, who died so we can live, and who was raised from death to life. All the Eritreans in that cell listened carefully and responded to the Holy Spirit's tugging on their hearts. They repeated the words of my call just before being transferred to another prison the very next morning. After that experience, when I finally embraced God's purpose for my imprisonment, I started to seize every opportunity to share the good news of the Gospel with my co-prisoners and as many other people as possible.

I recorded another experience in the letter, a similar one that had occurred only the week before. I was sitting in the chapel one morning when a young Sudanese man walked in, desperate to talk with me. Immediately, I stopped my reading of the Psalms and asked him about his relationship with God. As I listened to his answer, I sensed the Lord calling me to share the Gospel with him plainly, to invite this young man to accept Jesus Christ as his personal Lord and Savior. His name, coincidentally, was Abraham, and in a matter of minutes, he decided to follow in the footsteps of his namesake and give his life to Christ. When I started to read my Bible again that day and recorded the date, I realized it was the one-year anniversary of my imprisonment! The Lord was so great and so kind to let me crown my prison anniversary by leading another fellow prisoner to Christ!

Nearly every day, the Lord sent somebody into the chapel, and I heard the quiet voice of the Holy Spirit leading me, guiding me, and giving me the right words to say. The Lord's intentions are so very great, and I was thankful He "always leads us in triumphal procession, and through us spreads the fragrance of the knowledge of him everywhere" (2 Corinthians 2:14).

At the end of my letter, I included a final benediction for my family: "May the Lord bless and keep you all. With love, Petr."

29

It was Christmas Eve day—my second Christmas imprisoned in Sudan—and I was staring at more than two hundred prisoners who had squeezed into our chapel. We had to add more chairs and benches to accommodate them all. The prison authorities let us borrow loudspeakers, which the Sudanese Christians enjoyed singing through, and the noise even drew Muslims who would be sharing this Christmas holiday with us.

It was a very emotional service. Shortly before my sermon, I was able to call my family briefly from one of the functional toilets in the chapel. Hurrying, I told them I had only a few minutes to talk since I was about to preach that night.

We stayed in the chapel the whole night, praying and preparing for the next day, and in the morning, the local Catholic priest arrived at the chapel. For the first and only time in the history of Al-Huda Prison, one hundred men on death row were allowed to attend our chapel. These were men who were placed in the death cell—a holding cell for those about to be executed. Pastor Hassan and Pastor Kuwa visited the death cell every Sunday and preached to these men, but because I was a foreigner, the guards didn't allow me to join them.

On Christmas, I was finally able to meet the Christians from death row for the first time. With tears spilling from our eyes, we hugged each other. These men were destined to die, and I embraced them knowing they would likely be executed before we had the chance to meet again on earth.

We would see each other in Heaven soon enough.

| | | | | | |

At the end of December, I finally took the stand in my trial. The prosecutor questioned me, and I responded confidently.

"When did you visit Sudan?" he asked.

"I visited South Sudan in 2012, but I didn't enter Sudan and never met any military commanders."

"How did you enter Sudan in 2015?"

"I entered using a tourist visa."

"Do you work for VOM?"

"I have contract work with VOM," I explained, "but I'm not a VOM employee because I am not an American citizen."

"Why did you attend the conference in Addis Ababa?"

"I attended the conference in order to pray for peace in Sudan." Following more questions about my work, my visits to Sudan, and the help I offered to the injured Christian student, I concluded my testimony with a bold declaration. "In a normal country, when anyone from overseas brings funds to help someone, the government is thankful. I did not come to Sudan to engage in espionage; I came to help someone in need. Sudan should be grateful."

I knew my testimony was strong, but I also knew it would not be enough.

| | | | | | |

On Sunday, January 29, I awoke before dawn and prepared, once again, for the journey to Khartoum. Our trial had consisted of twenty-one court hearings spread over nearly six months. For the whole time, the Sudanese media had splashed propaganda news articles about my arrest all over their pro-government newspapers. I expected to be imprisoned a total of three months—a formality, really. But it was now January 2017, and I had been detained for more than a year.

Finally, my trial had come to an end. If nothing else, at least that would mean no more long, hot, dusty rides in the back of a cattle truck from Al-Huda to the courthouse in Khartoum. I packed my belongings into my carry-on suitcase and climbed, one final time, into the cattle truck.

Brother Monim consistently read the newspaper in prison. Most of our hearings happened on Sunday, and there would typically be a feature story about the case in either Monday's or Tuesday's newspaper. Monim would read the stories and then translate for me what was being said about our case. The stories were often illustrated with photos that had been taken from my hard drive—the government's "proof" that I was a spy.

Knowing what the newspapers—controlled by the government— were saying about our case, I felt there was no way we would simply be sentenced to the time we'd already served in prison and allowed to go home; the government had invested too much time and effort in painting us as dangerous criminals and spies. For the Sudanese government, it was important to be able to communicate to the world that their system of government and their Islamic laws against Christian activity were good and appropriate. I knew my arrest and imprisonment were political, and I awaited whatever my future held, even if that meant many more months—or even years—in prison. I knew that God was using me, and I trusted that He would use me further, whether in prison in Sudan or back home in the Czech Republic.

I talked with my family every night via my secret cell phone; I had prepared them for the likelihood that I would be found guilty. "Don't be surprised," I told them, "if I get sentenced to fifteen to twenty years in prison." But I also urged them not to be overwhelmed by the punishment. I reminded them we knew the Czech government was negotiating with Sudan on my behalf. As soon as the verdict was read and we knew what the punishment would be, I told them, everyone would know exactly what was at stake, and the negotiations could really get going!

In an earlier court session on January 2, 2017, the judge determined that Pastor Kuwa was not even in Khartoum at the same time I was and that he had only loaned his car to Pastor Hassan. So the case against Pastor Kuwa had been dismissed due to lack of evidence. My heart rejoiced for him, and I prayed that this was a sign of good news coming for us as well.

But Hassan, Monim, and I still awaited our verdicts, and on this day, we would receive them. We were silent as we walked into the court building, each of us thinking and praying, watching and waiting. I wondered what Vanda was doing back at home and prayed that the news I received today would not devastate her. We entered the courtroom and found it overflowing with activists, media, representatives of various embassies, and the general public. The judge entered, and we stood.

The judge's voice was firm and clear as he read from the prepared verdict document. Pastor Hassan and Monim were each found guilty of the four charges against them and sentenced to twelve years in prison. Pastor Hassan's teenaged daughter collapsed in tears behind us.

I had expected my verdict, but as the sentencing hearing was conducted entirely in Arabic, I was totally dependent on Pastor Hassan's translation. I sat on the bench, taking deep breaths, doing my best to calm my nerves, but I could feel my heart pounding in my chest. I focused my eyes on the judge and waited for him to speak. As he read my verdict, Hassan leaned over to me and relayed the words to me in English. He couldn't disguise the shock in his voice.

"The judge has found you guilty of all of the eight charges against you, and you have been given a life sentence in prison—the maximum short of the death penalty!"

As part of the sentence, I was also ordered to pay a fine of 100,000 Sudanese pounds (almost $17,000), and all my confiscated equipment—my Canon camera and lenses, laptop, iPhone, video camera, and external hard drives—became the property of the Sudanese government.

I was absolutely sure that my life was in the hands of the Lord, so I stayed calm. Though it might be hard to imagine, I felt *relief.* Though I had hoped and prayed for a better outcome, I was not entirely surprised that the Sudanese government had sentenced me to life in prison (which in Sudan amounted to a twenty-year sentence). The trial, the long ordeal, was finally over.

In one sense, this harsh penalty clearly showed the absurdity of the whole political and religious court case against me and my dear Sudanese fellow prisoners and brothers. If the government had made a more reasonable sentence—six months or one year—many people might have thought the charges were legitimate and that I really was involved in some criminal activity in Sudan. A life sentence for someone bringing aid into the country clearly showed that the entire trial had been a nonsensical farce.

As far as my possessions went, I was not worried about the material loss at all. I could buy a new computer or camera. The Lord had given, and the Lord had taken away; blessed be the name of the Lord (Job 1:21)! I was not even worried about the life sentence. After all, my life did not belong to me anymore—it belonged to Jesus Christ! He had bought it at a great price.

30

Pastor Hassan, Monim, and I no longer awaited our next court hearing in Khartoum. We were no longer the accused. Now, we were convicted criminals, and as such, we would be transferred to a new prison. Because of the flimsy evidence against them, Hassan and Monim were so certain of their release that they had already given away all their clothes and other belongings to prisoners at Al-Huda.

We spent the night after the verdict was announced in the transitional prison in Omdurman, crammed with dozens of men in the freezing cold, open-air holding cell. As criminals with long-term sentences, we were sent through the arduous process of being admitted and transferred to our final destination, which included having our fingerprints taken nearly a dozen times. After a bitter cold night outdoors, in the morning, we repeated the familiar routine of being loaded into the cattle truck. This time, though, we didn't know where we would end up. The uncertainty threatened to spill over into anxiety, but I reminded myself that the Lord was still in control.

The cattle truck snaked through the dusty city roads of Khartoum toward the airport, finally arriving at the Khartoum North Common Prison, known familiarly as "Kober prison." As we pulled up to the massive complex, I felt a strange mixture of apprehension and peace. I knew God was with me, but I had no way of knowing what would be in store at this final stop in the Sudanese prison system.

The main building of the compound was built in 1905 by a British man named Cooper, but when his surname was transcribed in Arabic, C-O-O-P-E-R became K-O-B-E-R. To me, the barred cell doors on both floors of Kober's main prison building looked like they had been transported straight from an American film set.

We were processed and then taken to separate sections of the prison. The guards took my MP3 player, and even though I kept my SIM card, I was forced to hand over my cell phone. I was terrified that they would confiscate my Bible, but remarkably, they allowed me to keep it. Hassan and I ended up in separate sections, both of which appeared to be in relatively good condition. I was glad to see that the toilets and showers in our area were in working order.

Monim, however, was not so fortunate. He was taken to the oldest part of the prison, the original building built by Mr. Cooper, and it was filthy and had no running water or functional toilet. Monim was from Darfur, and the Darfurians were viewed almost as traitors because of the civil war in Sudan. In addition, his darker skin likely made him an easy target for the racism that is common among many Arab Muslims in Sudan.

In recent years, Kober prison had been the site of some of Sudan's "ghost houses"—secret detention buildings where political prisoners were tortured physically and psychologically. Sometimes, they were executed. Prisoners were also transferred from the death cell of Al-Huda when the date of their execution arrived. Hassan and Monim learned of the hangings at Kober from the men on death row in Al-Huda, but we never saw them.

| | | | | | |

Kober prison had two kitchens—the first prepared food for its prisoners, and the other fed the inmates in the neighboring NISS prison. Because our food was cooked on site, the flat Sudanese bread we received each day was sometimes fresh and warm. Aside from the bread, the food in Kober was much better than the food in Al-Huda prison, where not even the Sudanese prisoners would eat the provided meals without resourcefully doctoring them on their prison-made electric stoves. But even in Kober, the prisoners were cooking the provided food further on. Like in Al-Huda, the prisoners in Kober who had some money were allowed to purchase a few items to eat, including wheat and sometimes even meat.

Pastor Hassan and I knew that some of our Muslim cellmates from Al-Huda had been transferred to Kober prison when they were caught swindling the prison guards. As punishment, they were sent to the strictest part of Kober. When we saw them, several days after Hassan, Monim, and I arrived, they rushed over and embraced me, wide smiles stretching across their faces. I quickly realized how much they appreciated and cherished our friendship, and I was again thankful that the Lord was using me in this way.

Often, the commander of the prison or his deputy made rounds to hear prisoner complaints. "I could have my MP3 player in Al-Huda," I said. "Why can't I have it here?" They promised me that I could—that I should ask my guard for it—but I never received it.

Even without the MP3 player, I continued to teach English in Kober. Using the Gospel of John, I taught my Muslim fellow prisoners the basics of the English language and prayed that the message of the Gospel was seeping into their hearts as well.

Unlike in the chapels of Omdurman and Al-Huda, I had only occasional opportunities to preach. Since I knew that some Muslims attended the chapel services, I made sure that my sermons were evangelistic. But with countless sermons from my Bible study in

Niyaba Mendola still untapped, I felt the loss of the regular opportunity to preach deep within my soul.

31

I gradually learned to get used to the conditions in Kober. I could still meet Pastor Hassan during the day, but after the afternoon attendance, we were locked in separate cells in different sections of the prison. In my so-called "VIP" section, I was imprisoned with convicted government officials, police officers, and security soldiers who defected from the battlefields in Darfur or even Yemen—men who had been sent to fight on behalf of Saudi Arabia at the behest of President Bashir. In the VIP section, there was even a colonel in Sudanese Security who refused to fulfill one such order.

These men were friendly to me and even shared with me the food their relatives brought to Kober. One of them even had an air-conditioned private cell, complete with satellite television. One day, the man was suffering from painful gout, and I gave him some of my ibuprofen tablets. He was grateful to finally have relief. When he realized I couldn't contact my family because I didn't have my phone, he gave me an open invitation to visit his air-conditioned room whenever I liked and use his phone to call my family. *Could this be a trap?* I wondered. At first I resisted his offer, but after a few long days, I gave in and called my wife.

The prison was very close to the airport, and from my cell, I could see planes taking off on a nearby runway. They were so close that I could see their wheels pull up at takeoff, and when I talked to Vanda at night, even she could hear the deafening roar of the enormous Russian cargo planes. My family had learned of my sentence from the consular officer from the Czech Embassy in Cairo, and though they were deeply disappointed, they had been prepared for the possibility. They hoped the diplomatic negotiations for my release would soon be successful, but they didn't know if the process would take weeks, months, or even years. Still, they fasted and prayed.

The imprisoned NISS soldiers in Kober spoke a bit of English and wanted me to teach them more, so with my Bible in hand, I used the Gospel of John as my textbook. There was a constant stream of soldiers, with many being released as soon as they agreed to return to battle.

Thankfully, my new friend in the air-conditioned cell didn't turn out to be a NISS spy, but during my time in prison, I encountered plenty of others who were. On the day we were sentenced, we were transferred to the transitional prison in Omdurman. While waiting in line for our fingerprints to be taken, I noticed a white man, slightly older than I was, and I greeted him in English. "Where are you from?" I asked.

At first, he put his finger to his lips, warning me to be quiet. Then, with a heavy Russian accent, he replied "No English." So, I repeated the same question in Russian, and he responded. He told me he was a mechanical engineer who had been cheated by a company that promised to provide a "good job" for him in Sudan. Eventually, the company representatives disappeared from Sudan, and all he was left with was an unpaid hotel bill.

The encounter was odd, and I was not entirely surprised when he accompanied me, Hassan, and Monim to Kober. Though he claimed not to speak English, he was always somehow around the three of us and always seemed eager to eavesdrop on our English conversations.

I felt uncomfortable with his presence, but I decided to share the Gospel with him in Russian. He immediately claimed to be a Russian Orthodox Christian!

One day, when he was loitering near us once again, an Egyptian prisoner recognized him as a Russian pilot who used to fly security soldiers from Khartoum to Darfur. Though this Egyptian spoke only a very little bit of broken English, he scared the Russian man to death by saying, "Anatolie . . . security . . . pilot" and pointing at his shoulders where his officer ranks would normally be displayed. The Russian pilot ran away as quickly as he could manage, and it was quite some time before we saw him again.

Brother Monim was only occasionally allowed to visit our section of Kober. During the day, I usually sat in the shade and read my Bible. As I was not allowed to go to the prison chapel very often, I decided to share the Gospel in French with some of my fellow prisoners from the francophone African countries. One young Muslim, a soccer player from Guinea, was especially eager to listen to my little sermons in French, and we became close friends. Each day, I prayed that the Lord would reveal Himself as Lord, Savior, and God to my young Muslim friend.

ı ı ı ı ı ı

Each day in Kober, I was reminded that my time and my life were in the Lord's hands. He was the one who was in control. During my daily routine one morning, as I sat under a courtyard tree and read from my favorite part of Scripture—the Psalms—I came to Psalm 126:

When the LORD restored the fortunes of Zion, we were like those who dream. Then our mouth was filled with laughter, and our tongue with shouts of joy; then they said among the nations, "The LORD has done great things for them."

The LORD has done great things for us; we are glad (Psalm 126:1–3).

Suddenly, two guards appeared in front of me with a startling message. Nothing they could have said would have surprised me more, and I struggled to understand the news.

"Petr," they said, "you are being released from prison today!"

The feeling just described in Psalm 126 washed over me. *Is this real?* I wondered. *Isn't this a dream?* I had been fooled many times before, and it was hard to believe that this could be anything but a dream. But the news was, in fact, real! Tears sprang to my eyes, and I thought of Vanda. *Finally!*

Word of my release spread like fire among all the prisoners in our section. As happened any time a prisoner was released, the news offered the prison a moment of joy and celebration. *Perhaps next time it will be me*, each man would think. Joyful shouts radiated from my fellow prisoners, and they wrapped me in exuberant hugs. Soon, I saw Hassan and Monim rushing toward me, and they were rejoicing as well: if I was being released, then they would surely be released soon as well.

As was customary, I donated my clothing to the other prisoners. The men reached eagerly for my few belongings, and I carefully oversaw the chaotic distribution process, just to make sure Hassan and Monim received my medicines. The guards were waiting, though, and I knew I had to leave. With only a small, half-empty carry-on in my hand, I followed them to the prison reception area.

Two security officers from the NISS were waiting for me. "The President of Sudan has granted you pardon," they announced. "From now on, you are a free man."

I glanced down at the guns underneath their shirts. Despite the fact that I was leaving prison, I was very aware that I was still in Sudan, under the absolute control of a totalitarian regime that could do anything it pleased. A dull sense of anxiety was just below the surface of my emotions, and I was on high alert. President Bashir had been in power for nearly three decades, and I knew this newfound purported "freedom" may not yet mean I was truly free.

The prison guards returned my valuables, including my MP3 player and cell phone. My SIM card was still carefully hidden in the secret pocket of my underwear.

"You will come with us," they said.

32

I watched apprehensively as the officers put my carry-on suitcase into the back of a small white car and then drove me to a barber shop, where they insisted my beard be shaved. The barber had me lean back in the chair and then covered my face with a soothing treatment mask. The process struck me as an absurd attempt to impress—to prove that I had been cared for well while in Sudanese custody. He repeated the procedure three times, and my body began to ache from sitting in the same uncomfortable position for such a long time. When he was satisfied with the series of facial treatments, he hurried off to find a small, mobile massager with which to relieve the tension in my neck and shoulders.

"You have to relax," the officers told me as we finally left the barber. This was certainly easier said than done. I was in the presence of the same NISS officers who had interrogated me and admitted me to prison, and their very appearance took me back to some of the worst and lowest moments of the past fifteen months. Even more importantly, I could see their guns underneath their shirts.

"We're going to take you to the sauna," they said.

I had no interest in going to the sauna—it would only give the officers a chance to search my bags for my cell phone—but my new-found "freedom" mandated that I go. I didn't want to make any trouble, so I went along without complaint. We arrived at a private sauna, and I walked into the changing room.

As I undressed, I folded my clothes neatly on my bag and pulled out my cell phone. In a matter of minutes, they would begin searching everything I had. I couldn't take the cell phone with me into the sauna, but I also couldn't allow them to take my SIM card—the tiny chip contained all the information of my prison phone calls and messages. So, I quickly took it from the secret pocket in my underwear and slid it into my mouth, tucking it securely behind my back molar.

I spent ten restless minutes in the hot sauna before insisting we leave.

The officers drove me to a local fast-food restaurant where they ordered me a large meal of fried chicken legs, French fries, salad, and Sprite, and watched as I tried to eat. My stomach was sensitive, and much smaller, from over a year of meager rations, and besides, I felt awkward eating with such an attentive audience.

We left the restaurant and drove to a posh clothing store. "Do you want to buy cologne? A suit? You need a shirt and tie." One of the men shuffled a huge stack of money.

No way, I thought. *I'm in Africa. I'm not traveling in a suit.*

I could see that my minders had been ordered to make me look as good as possible. If I was set free looking like a well-dressed businessman walking out of a luxury hotel, how could the world possibly complain that I'd been mistreated? I tried, without angering my guards, to avoid cooperating in this bit of theater.

"I have good clothes," I said.

"No, no, your clothes are not good enough." They seemed to have more information than I did.

Chapter Thirty-Two

"I have these jeans," I said, and I showed them some clean clothes in my suitcase. They had been given strict instructions to make me presentable, but reluctantly, the officers settled for purchasing me a belt to replace the tattered plastic string holding up my trousers.

Next, we traveled to a grocery store. They told me to buy enough food for three or four days of breakfast, so I picked up instant coffee, tea, bread, eggs, fruit, and chocolate bars.

We loaded once more into the vehicle, and soon arrived at what appeared to be an apartment building. A huge, concrete wall topped with barbed wire surrounded the structure, and German shepherds barked menacingly from behind the fence as we exited the car. The NISS officers walked me inside. I would stay here until Monday, they said: four nights. They took my best T-shirt to the dry cleaners—it was the one I had been saving for my trip home—and promised to return it shortly.

My SIM card was still in my mouth.

I I I I I I

The officers left, and I was finally alone in my bedroom in the apartment. I knew it was bugged, but I had to call Vanda. I glanced quickly around the apartment and determined that the bathroom was likely the most private area, so I walked over to the toilet, slipped the SIM card from my mouth, dried it on my shirt, slid it back into the cell phone, and quickly dialed Vanda's number.

Back at home in the Czech Republic, Vanda answered the phone. My voice was a whisper, and I had to talk quickly.

"What's going on?" Vanda asked anxiously.

"I was released from Kober prison this morning, and now I'm in an unknown location," I whispered. "It looks like an off-the-books stash-house of the Sudanese secret police. I've been told that I'll stay here for some time." Officials in Czechoslovakia kept such apartments or homes during Communist times there; it was a secret place where they could hide a person, meet with a source, interrogate a prisoner, or take a mistress without being discovered.

Vanda was confused by this mysterious phone call and concerned that I was in danger. Growing up under Communism in Czechoslovakia, she knew many stories of political prisoners who would be "released" from prison only to be found dead. It was the way the government fixed those cases, and now she feared that Sudan's leaders might be trying to "fix" my case as well.

We hung up the phone and Vanda, with competing emotions of excitement and worry, began to pray.

33

For three nights, I stayed in the NISS apartment and waited. I lay on the bed all day, listened to Scripture on my MP3 player, and wondered what would happen next.

The apartment was small, with one large bed inside a single bedroom. The bed smelled clean, so I decided to lean back on the coverlet. The apartment had running water for only a few minutes each day, so I left a bucket under an open tap in the dirty bathroom and waited for the pipes to open. When the bucket filled, I used a plastic bottle to shower and dried myself with the provided towels. Sometimes at night, I heard the sound of the running water and jumped from my bed to flush the toilet.

During the night, the security officers checked on me every half an hour, making sure I hadn't escaped. "Would you like us buy you some wine?" they asked. "Or call you some ladies?" I declined their offers of alcohol and prostitutes, but I soon learned there were other visitors to my apartment. When I turned off the light at night, mice jumped from the floor right onto my bed. Sometimes, they landed either on me or on my pillow, right behind my freshly shaved head. I leaped from my bed and turned on the light, and the mice immediately disappeared. The next morning, as I investigated, searching the apartment for their entryway, I learned that they were coming up from the sewer system in the bathtub.

Between the rodents and the guards, I hardly slept, but I did manage to take a nap each afternoon. The guards had been given orders to keep me well fed, so twice we went out to eat. The rest of the time, I ate the food they bought me at the grocery store. On the gas stove, I boiled water for tea and cooked eggs, waiting for Monday to come.

| | | | | | |

At 3:30 p.m. on Sunday, February 26, the day before I was scheduled to leave, the security officers arrived at my apartment and announced, "Someone wants to talk to you, so get ready." I had kept my things packed in case I needed to be able to move at a moment's notice, so I grabbed my suitcase and walked toward the door. *Finally!*

"No, no, calm down," one of the men said. "Someone wants to talk to you on the phone." I put down my luggage and he passed me a cell phone.

I was astonished to hear the voice of the Czech ambassador on the line.

"Mr. Jašek," she said, "where are you? We've come to pick you up. We're waiting at the airport for you." I was so happy that I could hardly speak.

"That's so good!" I said, but I didn't know where I was, and I wondered how I would get to the airport.

"We are scheduled to leave at 5:00 p.m.," the ambassador replied. But I knew we were not close to the airport, and I doubted I would be able to make it there in time to leave. There was less than an hour and a half before the flight would depart, and I was at the mercy of my NISS handlers.

I hung up the phone, the security officers left, and I waited. I was alone in the apartment, watching the minutes tick by. It felt like an eternity. A little after 4:00 p.m., they finally returned, but by that time, I was certain I would miss the flight.

We loaded into the vehicle and began the journey to the Khartoum airport. I didn't have a passport or any other form of identification. I wondered if the Sudanese would already have at least one of my passports at the airport, since I'd arrived in Khartoum with two. I wondered briefly about my computer, my camera, and my other possessions. If it was true that I'd received a full pardon, then it was supposed to be as if I'd never committed a crime. And that would mean that the punishment of forfeiting these items would be erased … at least in theory. But I didn't want to risk offending my guards by asking about these things. (Pardon or no, I have never seen those items since my trial. There is probably an officer in the NISS taking wonderful photos with my old camera!)

I thought of my ride in the hotel shuttle bus fifteen months earlier, and I prayed that this trip would end much differently than that one did.

I I I I I I

Finally, we arrived at the airport. My security guards were dressed in plain clothes and sunglasses, and I soon realized they were masquerading as airport employees. The security guards presented badges and ushered us into a secure area of the airport. Then they opened my car door and escorted me into a VIP lounge. Czech Intelligence officers, one of them a man I'd met a year earlier in the NISS National Club, were waiting for me, along with two physicians.

Two NISS security officers followed me through the lounge. One of them I recognized from the NISS prison—he was the man who had taken my mugshots when I was arrested.

The physicians had come prepared with what looked like a complete field hospital. They conducted a full physical exam, connected me to an ECG machine, measured my oxygen, and offered me special rehydration drinks with electrolytes. They had learned from the Czech consular officer that I was behaving normally and that my mind seemed intact, but they were concerned about the possibility of dehydration. The two NISS officers stared at me in astonishment. I was sure they were convinced by the immense attention of the Czech Intelligence physicians that I surely must have been a spy.

Following my exam, we waited. I learned that the Czech Minister of Foreign Affairs would soon be arriving and that we would be returning to Prague on his plane. "I need to go to the restroom," I managed to say.

In the restroom, I pulled out my cell phone and quietly called Vanda. After the fear-inducing phone call three days earlier, she was relieved to hear my voice again. Vanda had been following the Minister of Foreign Affairs' travel schedule on his official website and knew he had left for a one-day trip to Sudan on the twenty-sixth. If the trip went according to plan, she knew I could be back home in a matter of hours.

"I am in the airport," I said eagerly, "and it looks as if we will be flying soon. We are waiting for the minister and his team."

I soon realized my phone call had been a risk. When we received word that the Minister of Foreign Affairs was en route, we left the lounge. Sudanese guards accompanied us all the way to the stairs of the aircraft, which was an enormous official plane belonging to the Czech government. We boarded the plane, and I asked to make another phone call to my wife.

"Better not, please," the Intelligence officer said. "You actually made a big mistake calling your wife from the restroom." The shaky negotiations for my release hadn't been finalized until just the day before, he said, and the officers knew that until I was actually in the air, anything was possible.

I leaned back into the plush leather airplane seat with the sobering realization that I could have just jeopardized my own release.

Within forty-five minutes, the Minister of Foreign Affairs arrived, together with his company. I was somewhat concerned about how he would welcome me. I had heard from my family that he'd once said publicly I must have expected trouble when documenting the violation of the rights of persecuted Christians in Sudan. In one sense, I felt like he'd implied everything I'd endured had been my fault because I had decided to travel to a country as dangerous as Sudan.

Minister Lubomír Zaorálek entered the airplane, smiled at me, and said, "Mr. Jašek, welcome on board the Czech Air Force airplane! First of all, I would like to pass greetings from my friends of the Bretheren Church in Most who told me a lot about your humanitarian work. I really appreciate the work you are doing." The ice broke completely. I shook his hand and then was welcomed by his staff members and spokesman.

Our flight to Prague took slightly more than six hours. During that time, Minister Zaorálek left his seat in business class to sit with me in the back. For about two hours, he asked me in detail about my horrible prison experience. He listened quietly, then turned to me and said something that revealed a deep understanding of what I'd been through and summarized what I had hoped would be true throughout the previous year:

"Man, as I am listening to you, I bet that your model must be the Apostle Paul."

34

On the evening of February 26, Vanda's phone rang once more. The Czech consular officer, Jaroslav Vejrych, was on the other end of the line with wonderful news: "Petr is on the plane."

Vanda burst into tears and hugged our children tightly. They praised the Lord and began urgently spreading the good news among the Christians who had prayed and fasted for me for fourteen long months.

My family knew I would be landing at the military airport in Prague but that they wouldn't be able to see me there. They drove to the military hospital and waited eagerly.

When I stepped off the plane hours later, a crowd of reporters had gathered for a press conference. Into the sea of microphones, I had a chance to thank the Minister of Foreign Affairs for his hard, consistent work in negotiating my release. I understood how difficult this must have been, I continued, in a country where the president had charges pending against him from the International Criminal Court. I expressed my deep appreciation for my home church in Kladno and our pastor, Daniel Kaleta. I thanked the US representatives from VOM for their great support of me, my lawyer, and especially my family during this difficult time. Finally, I thanked the hundreds of thousands of Christians who had been praying for me and those who had signed the online petition of CitizenGo, an organization that campaigns for persecuted people around the world.

While I stood on the tarmac in Prague and while I was being transported to the military hospital for observation, my heart and mind were still in Sudan. Shortly after midnight, when I stepped from the ambulance and my family leapt from their car and rushed toward me—while I wrapped them in my arms for the first time in over a year—I thanked the Lord that we are part of an even larger family. It is one that spans the globe, and I thanked God that not even a Sudanese prison could separate us from one another.

Epilogue

When I returned to Prague, surrounded once again by my family and our church family who prayed for me so fervently while I was in Sudan, I began reflecting on how God had changed me over the fourteen and a half months of my imprisonment.

I was so thankful to the Lord—deeply thankful—for allowing me the privilege of suffering dishonor for the name of my Savior. For my family's sake, I was thankful that my arrest happened when my children were already grown so they could encourage my wife, Vanda, who I think suffered the most. But for my own sake, I wished God had allowed this experience to happen earlier because I know the rest of my life would have looked so much different.

God often allows suffering to teach us patience, to teach us how to wait on Him. The Psalmist wrote, "I wait for the Lord, my soul waits, and in his word I hope" (Psalm 130:5). Waiting for the Lord is the key to the Christian life. It unlocks all the Christian disciplines like prayer, fasting, and serving others, and it cures us from suffering from an "instant Christianity"—an attitude that I had encountered in my own heart during the first part of my imprisonment.

In March 2016, when I thought I was going to be released, I felt frustrated with God for keeping me in prison. I wanted to go home to be with my family. I wanted to go back to my church in the Czech Republic and worship with them like before. But after prison, I saw the situation in a different way. The Lord had better things in store for me. He was keeping me in Sudan for a reason. He was preparing me to preach the Gospel at Omdurman Prison, at Al-Huda Prison, at Kober, and to show the love of God to my interrogators and lawyers in the court proceedings. God's timing is always better than our own. When I stopped thinking about myself, I stopped feeling miserable, and I saw a larger plan taking shape.

For me, my experiences in prison in Sudan were a profound opportunity to proclaim Christ, even if it brought personal pain. I have learned that God sometimes allows us to "walk through the valley of the shadow of death" (Psalm 23:4) to teach us to trust in His strength instead of trusting in our own. It is only in the valley, in the shadows, in the darkness, that we see Christ shining the brightest. The more helpless, hopeless, and defenseless we are, the more our ears are tuned to the voice of the Shepherd as His rod, His staff, and His footprints lead the way.

There were many times, especially as my health was failing at the NISS prison, when I felt frustrated because I couldn't find the right words to pray. Sometimes, while being beaten by my ISIS cellmates, all I could do was groan. But during those awful moments, the Holy Spirit was groaning with me, interceding on my behalf (Romans 8:26).

Four months after my arrest, when God gave me the opportunity to share the Gospel with twelve Eritreans, I had a complete change of mind. Up until that time, all I could think about was going home and being free, but as I began telling those men about the love of Christ and saw them respond in obedience to God, I suddenly realized: *What are four months in prison compared to an eternity in Heaven?*

At that moment, my attitude shifted. I began thinking less about my circumstances and more about the men who needed Christ. God was showing me the importance of seeing life from a taller perspective, from an eternal perspective.

Sudan made me more grateful for the Bible than I ever was in the Czech Republic. The Holy Spirit always speaks to us when we read His Word. I felt this most acutely when the consular of the Czech Embassy gave me a Bible to read. When I took it back to my cell and read it cover to cover, I developed an appetite for God's Word unlike anything I had ever experienced. The presence of Christ was immediate, powerful, and real in my cell.

The more I read of God's Word, the hungrier I became to know God more. I finally understood more fully what Paul meant when he wrote, "For this light momentary affliction is preparing for us an eternal weight of glory beyond all comparison, as we look not to the things that are seen but to the things that are unseen. For the things that are seen are transient, but the things that are unseen are eternal" (2 Corinthians 4:17–18). I finally understood how the Psalmist must have felt when he declared, "The Lord has become my stronghold, and my God the rock of my refuge" (Psalm 94:22). During those deep, intense times of Bible reading, I prepared more sermons than I was able to preach, and to this day, I still haven't preached them all.

The Word of God is not chained (2 Timothy 2:9)—even when God's people are. The Scripture is alive and active, and when I began feeling its activity in prison, I could not keep it to myself. The Lord began prodding me to share the Gospel with my fellow prisoners—nominal Christians, animists, and even Muslims. The Lord gave me the privilege not only to preach the Gospel in various prisons, but also to express love to my fellow prisoners, many of whom were enemies of the Gospel only because they had never really heard it before. With the Lord's grace, I was able to plant the seed of God's truth into their hearts, and I pray that other people may water it and that the Lord will cause it to grow. In prison, I truly learned to love my enemies. I still pray for the ISIS prisoners, and I pray that the many

Christian prisoners in Sudan might have the opportunity to share the Gospel as well.

Early in my life, I always wondered how someone could do the work of a pastor. I once told my wife, "Being a pastor is a very demanding role. How can someone prepare sermons every Sunday and say new things without sounding repetitive? I could never be a pastor." I couldn't imagine preparing sermons every Sunday, but in prison, when I was spending time with the Lord every day, doing the work of a pastor became a very natural thing. The Holy Spirit was teaching me how to listen to His voice.

Above all, this experience in prison sensitized me even more to the importance of prayer. I sometimes hear people casually say, "I will pray for you." I once talked like that, too. But do I really pray? How frequently? For how long? I have a friend in the former Soviet Union, a man named Anatolie, who wakes up and prays for me every morning.

When I was first arrested in Sudan, my wife had very little information about me. The first person my family called was our pastor. Immediately, a prayer chain started, and about three weeks later, a fasting chain started. Every day, at least one person—and sometimes as many as three different people—were fasting the entire day and praying for me.

Under normal circumstances, my family would attend Bible study once a week. While I was in Sudan, though, my wife attended at least two, sometimes even three different Bible study groups. One evening, the elder leading a Bible study group closed his Bible and told the others that the Holy Spirit was leading him to stop discussing their particular Scripture passage and instead get on their knees to pray for me and the situation I found myself in at that very moment in my cell. The whole group dropped to their knees and began to declare the Lord's victory in the cell where I was. After they finished praying, the group peacefully returned home.

It was only months later, after I was released from prison and was sitting in our living room reviewing the family calendar with my wife, that I made an astonishing discovery. As Vanda and I shared with each other what we had experienced with the Lord on each day of my imprisonment, we discovered that on the day of the intentional Bible study group prayer, I was on my knees before the ISIS cellmates as they interrogated and beat me with the broomstick. At the moment I needed prayer maybe more than I have needed it at any other time in my life, the Lord Himself was raising up prayer warriors to battle with me and for me. The Lord is great, and the Holy Spirit intercedes for the saints according to the will of God (Romans 8:27). Praise the Lord for this wonderful confirmation!

This experience in prison taught me all over again the value of interceding for other Christians around the world. Like Aaron and Hur who held up the arms of Moses during battle, we must also support those who are struggling and suffering, those who are being persecuted right now, today, at this very moment. I spent many hours praying for Pastor Hassan and Monim after my release. Both men were eventually freed, but my heart continues to remain with my brothers in prison in Sudan, and I occasionally still hear from many of them via email and text. God's people *must* be a people of prayer.

God's kingdom never spreads like we expect it will. The Lord chooses to use weak and broken things—cracked vessels— to transport His life-changing message. If God could use someone like me to spread the Gospel, He can also use someone like you.

For me, I pray that my experiences will encourage all of my Christian brothers and sisters around the world who are facing persecution or who may face persecution one day soon. People often ask me if I think of myself as a martyr. I am no martyr, but I have seen the faces of the people who are—faces like Monica, Danjuma, and so many of the Christians I met in the Sudanese prisons.

In Philippians 1:29, Paul says to the church in Philippi, "For it has been granted to you that for the sake of Christ you should not only believe in him but also suffer for his sake." I have studied that verse in different translations of the Bible, and one translation specifically says that it has been granted as a "privilege" not only to believe in Christ but also to suffer for His sake.

When my family still lived under Communism, my brother and sister and I traveled to Great Britain, the furthest we could go at that time by car—taking the ferry across the English Channel. We visited a church north of London and attended a Bible study. Right at the time, the group was discussing persecution and suffering, and suddenly there we were, three people from Communist Czechoslovakia.

The group asked us how we viewed persecution. At that time, we probably could have been considered the experts on it in that small Bible study group. I remember the first words my sister Jana said: "I believe that it is a privilege to suffer for the Lord." The pastor understood immediately, but the others were confused. What kind of privilege could it possibly be to experience persecution?

I have experienced personally the *privilege* of persecution, and I am only grateful for the opportunity to share, even a little, in Jesus Christ's suffering.

The Gospel of Jesus Christ is the persecution gospel, and the Lord Jesus prepared His disciples for persecution in John 15:18-21:

> If the world hates you, know that it has hated me before it hated you. If you were of the world, the world would love you as its own; but because you are not of the world, but I chose you out of the world, therefore the world hates you. Remember the word that I said to you: "A servant is not greater than his master." If they persecuted me, they will also persecute you. If they kept my word, they will also keep yours. But all these things they will do to you on account of my name, because they do not know him who sent me.

In Luke 21:12–16, the Lord gives us more details about the coming persecution:

But before all this they will lay their hands on you and persecute you, delivering you up to the synagogues and prisons, and you will be brought before kings and governors for my name's sake. This will be your opportunity to bear witness. Settle it therefore in your minds not to meditate beforehand how to answer, for I will give you a mouth and wisdom, which none of your adversaries will be able to withstand or contradict. You will be delivered up even by parents and brothers and relatives and friends, and some of you they will put to death.

Yes, some of us Christians will be put to death. Paul reminds us of this in Romans 8:35–39:

Who shall separate us from the love of Christ? Shall tribulation, or distress, or persecution, or famine, or nakedness, or danger, or sword? As it is written, "For your sake we are being killed all the day long; we are regarded as sheep to be slaughtered." No, in all these things we are more than conquerors through him who loved us. For I am sure that neither death nor life, nor angels nor rulers, nor things present nor things to come, nor powers, nor height nor depth, nor anything else in all creation, will be able to separate us from the love of God in Christ Jesus our Lord.

When I dare to think about Christians being slaughtered in large numbers every year in Northern Nigeria, I am often reminded of the fact that we Christians "are regarded as sheep to be slaughtered." But from the eternal perspective, in all these things, we are more than conquerors!

With these words, spoken long before my prison pulpit, I offered the encouragement of Christ to many Christians around the world. I was preparing them for persecution with Paul's words from 2 Timothy 3:12: "Indeed, all who desire to live a godly life in Christ Jesus will be persecuted." I actively encouraged others to get ready for persecution, so how could I be surprised to face it myself?

The Lord has granted me *the privilege* to suffer for the sake of His name, and there is great joy in being counted worthy of that calling.

Afterword

A Word About Suffering

Perhaps you thought about the meaning of suffering when hearing about the dramatic forms of persecution experienced by Christians in Sudan. I hope you'll agree with me that persecution is not only a "disciplinary instrument" for lukewarm Christians to let them get rid of their carnality or a "catalyst" to spread the Gospel.

The New Testament speaks about suffering from a different point of view: "But rejoice insofar as you share Christ's sufferings, that you may also rejoice and be glad when his glory is revealed" (1 Peter 4:13). Yes, you read properly: we should *rejoice* when sharing in sufferings! Look at the apostles who were being beaten by the Jews: "Then they left the presence of the council, rejoicing that they were counted worthy to suffer dishonor for the name" of Jesus (Acts 5:41). Yes, the apostles considered it *an honor* to be beaten for their Lord.

In Philippians 1:29, the apostle Paul considers the suffering of the Christians a "granted privilege": "For it has been granted to you that for the sake of Christ you should not only believe in him but also suffer for his sake." I believe that suffering, especially when crowned with a martyr's death, is one of the outstanding honors and an important privilege for Christians. This "graduation ceremony" includes a lot of spectators. But they don't only include demanding spectators of the Roman arenas or furious members of the executing commandos. (By the way, some of these became genuine Christians when seeing the faithfulness of the executed Christians.) Christian martyrs are a testimony of faith and obedience not only to our visible world, but—I dare to say—especially to the spiritual one. "For I think that God has exhibited us apostles as last of all, like men sentenced to death, because we have become a spectacle [Greek: *theatron*] to the world, to angels, and to men" (1 Corinthians 4:9). Yes, a theater! Of course, it is pertinent for Christians to be ready to appear on life's stage, or—as you like—in the arena on public display.

I know the Lord is proud of His servants—He even prides Himself on them. "Have you considered My servant Job, that there is none like him on the earth, a blameless and upright man, one who fears God and shuns evil?" says the Lord to Satan. It isn't Satan who, with malicious joy, would point to the chosen object of his temptation, whom he knows about and whom he will dupe. It's the Lord who prides Himself on His servant because He knows Job will remain faithful even in the most difficult temptations. He knows what we are able to bear, and He will not allow us to be tempted beyond that (see 1 Corinthians 10:13).

Yes, a Christian martyr is a "live" actor on the stage of ages over which the Lord Himself is the director, and the spectator in the first row of seats is Satan with his servants. God demonstrates to the visible as well as to the spiritual world the faithfulness of His servants, which Lucifer lost when he lifted himself up in pride.

The Lord doesn't choose that role for everyone to play. Nonetheless, we are one body in Christ. "If one member suffers, all suffer together; if one member is honored, all rejoice together" (1 Corinthians 12:26).

As we are members of one body, it is fully natural to be interested in *where* and *how* a part of our body—our brothers and sisters—suffers.

"Remember those who are in prison, as though in prison with them, and those who are mistreated, since you also are in the body" (Hebrew 13:3). We can understand the word "body" not only as a physical body, but also as a spiritual body—the church. By refusing to be unconcerned or indifferent toward our persecuted Christian brothers and sisters—wherever they live around the world—we make it clear that we are fundamentally affected by their sufferings, that we are members of the same body, of which the Lord Jesus Christ is the head.

"I was in prison and you came to me," says the Lord Himself in Matthew 25:36. It's almost impossible to visit the majority of totalitarian prisons. Nevertheless, what we can do is send an encouraging card to the prisoner or a protest card to their prison guard. There are many ways to show how we are members of the same suffering body, and the Lord wants us to do that.

About the Author

I n 2002, Petr Jašek joined The Voice of the Martyrs (VOM) to help aid and assist persecuted Christians in hostile areas and restricted nations. With a background in hospital administration, he oversaw VOM's work in Africa. As Petr traveled to meet with persecuted believers, he encouraged them with stories from his own experience growing up as the son of a pastor who was persecuted in Communist Czechoslovakia.

Petr's life changed dramatically in December 2015 when he was arrested at the airport in Khartoum, Sudan. He had just met with Christians to evaluate how VOM could best serve them. Instead of continuing his work with imprisoned believers and their families, Petr became a prisoner himself.

Petr had times of discouragement in prison, but he also found God's faithfulness to be real and true. He turned his imprisonment into an opportunity to grow in Christ, sharing his faith with others and encouraging the Christians imprisoned with him.

Throughout his 445 days in prison, VOM and Christians around the world stood with Petr's family through prayer and other means of support. When Petr was released, he returned to his wife, Vanda, and two grown children in the Czech Republic.

Petr continues to work with VOM, serving as the ministry's global ambassador and traveling around the world to speak about his time in prison and to encourage believers to stand with our persecuted brothers and sisters in prayer and action.

About
The Voice of the Martyrs

The Voice of the Martyrs (VOM) is a nonprofit, interdenominational Christian missions organization dedicated to serving our persecuted family worldwide through practical and spiritual assistance and leading other members of the body of Christ into fellowship with them. VOM was founded in 1967 by Pastor Richard Wurmbrand and his wife, Sabina. Richard was imprisoned fourteen years in Communist Romania for his faith in Christ, and Sabina was imprisoned for three years. They were ransomed out of Romania in 1965 and soon established a global network of missions dedicated to assisting persecuted Christians.

To be inspired by the courageous faith of our persecuted brothers and sisters in Christ who are advancing the gospel in hostile areas and restricted nations, request a free subscription to VOM's award-winning monthly magazine. Visit us at vom.org, or call 800-747-0085.

To learn more about VOM's work, please contact us:

United States .... vom.org

Australia .... vom.com.au

Belgium .... hvk-aem.be

Brazil.. maisnomundo.org

Canada.. vomcanada.com

Czech Republic .... hlas-mucedniku.cz

Finland .... marttyyrienaani.fi

Germany.. verfolgte-christen.org

The Netherlands .... sdok.nl

New Zealand .... vom.org.nz

Poland.. gpch.pl

Portugal .... vozdosmartires.com

Singapore .... gosheninternational.org

South Africa... persecutionsa.org

South Korea .... vomkorea.kr

United Kingdom .... releaseinternational.org